The HOLY SPIRIT *and the* INCORRUPTIBLE SEED

MARC BAKER

TWO BLESSED BEARS PUBLISHING
Bradenton, FL

The Holy Spirit and the Incorruptible Seed
ISBN: 979-8-9887462-0-1
Copyright © 2023 by Marc Baker
Bradenton, FL 34203

Published by:
Two Blessed Bears Publishing, LLC
Bradenton, FL 34203

Printed in the United States of America. All rights reserved under International Copyright Law. Contents and/or cover may not be reproduced in whole or in part without the express written consent of the Publisher.

All Scripture quotations are taken from the New King James Version® Copyright © 1982 by Thomas Nelson. Used by permission. All rights reserved.

Contents

1. Religious Tradition and the Works of Jesus 5
2. Unbelief, Relationship, and the Works of Jesus 13
3. Stepping Out in Faith to Do the Works of Jesus 21
4. Natural or Genuine Belief? 29
5. Why Are We Not Walking in the Power of
   the Early Church? 35
6. Have We Become Complacent? 41
7. Believe God's Word or Religious Tradition 49
8. Turn Your Eyes to the Spiritual Realm and Victory
   Will Follow 57
9. Meditation on God's Word Will Deepen Your
   Relationship with Him 63
10. Making the Word of God the Focus of Your Meditation ... 71
11. A Foundation in God's Word Will Lead to
    Spiritual Success 77
12. God Speaks to Us through His Word 81
13. Allowing the Word of God to Dominate Our Lives 87
14. Harnessing Our Imaginations with God's Word 93
15. Satan Seeks to Steal the Word from Our Hearts 99
16. Following the Spirit as We Sow the Seeds of God's Word ... 105

17. The Word Becomes Power If We Do Not Allow Satan
    to Steal It 111

18. The Word Must Take Root in Your Heart to Release Power . . 117

19. God's Word Alone Is the Seed That Produces Miracles 123

20. Who Is Trying to Shake Your Commitment to God's Word? 129

21. Pursuing Deep Roots in God's Word through Meditation . . . 137

22. Total Commitment to God's Word Provides Protection
    from the Storms 145

23. Press into God's Love by Praying in the Spirit 151

24. Press into Revelation Knowledge by Praying in the Spirit . . . 157

25. Are We Relying on Acquired or Revelation Knowledge? 165

26. Accessing the Mind of Christ through the Holy Spirit 171

27. Partnering with the Holy Spirit in Prayer to Draw
    from His Well of Perfect Knowledge 177

28. Speaking God's Words to Release His Power 183

29. God's Word Is an Unchanging and Eternal Covenant 189

30. God's Word and the Anointing 195

31. Plant the Word and Defend It 203

Chapter 1

Religious Tradition and the Works of Jesus

"Most assuredly, I say to you, he who believes in Me, the works that I do he will do also; and greater works than these he will do, because I go to My Father."

JOHN 14:12

In the fourteenth through seventeenth chapters of his Gospel, John provides us with Jesus' final words before His arrest. How many have read these chapters without understanding what the Lord said? I have read them for over thirty years and still find new truths.

Revelation Knowledge or Acquired Knowledge

You will find numerous mentions of revelation knowledge in this book. This term refers to knowledge that the Holy Spirit imparts. It differs from acquired knowledge, which one gains through personal effort. For instance, students may spend hours studying their textbooks and class notes to acquire enough knowledge to pass an exam.

Revelation knowledge is not acquired through our efforts. We see an example of this in a statement made by Paul in his letter to the Galatian Christians. He explains that God revealed His Son to him

(Galatians 1:15–16), so he did not consult with other people about what he had been shown. Instead, he sought guidance from the Holy Spirit and received it.

Before his conversion to Christianity, Paul was a prominent leader among the Jewish people. He boasted in Galatians of having surpassed many of his peers in his understanding of Judaism (Galatians 1:14). However, when it came to his Christian ministry, the knowledge he had obtained wasn't enough. Only the Holy Spirit could give him the knowledge he needed to flourish in his new role.

Jesus Prepared His Disciples for the Crucifixion

Jesus gave His final discourse to His disciples to prepare them for His crucifixion. He began by telling them not to let their hearts be troubled, as He knew His time with them was ending (John 14:1). The disciples expected Jesus to establish His earthly kingdom and free Israel from Rome, but instead, they were about to witness His arrest and crucifixion. Jesus was preparing them for this challenging time, and in John 14:2–3, He turned their attention to heaven and what He would be doing to prepare for their eventual reunion. His instructions show us that the cure for worry is to focus our attention on God instead of on the situations of life, and we will explore this further in the pages ahead.

The Religious Mindset

In John 14:4, Jesus assured His disciples that they would know how to follow Him when necessary. However, Thomas expressed doubts about this statement:

> Thomas said to Him, "Lord, we do not know where You are going, and how can we know the way?" (John 14:5)

Thomas relied on his understanding since he did not possess the Holy Spirit, and we can only comprehend spiritual truths with the guidance of the Holy Spirit. Just like the disciples, we cannot grasp it on our own.

I have highlighted the distinction between acquired and revelation knowledge. According to John 14:26, Jesus informed His disciples that the Holy Spirit would serve as their teacher. As Thomas had not yet received the Holy Spirit, he had to rely solely on acquired knowledge while listening to Jesus. Consequently, his comprehension of the Lord's teachings was restricted.

This book frequently mentions religious teaching, which refers to knowledge gained through personal effort. Jesus once warned the scribes and Pharisees that traditions could undermine the power of God's Word in our lives (Mark 7:13). These traditions arise when we try to interpret Scripture with our intellect rather than rely on the teaching ministry of the Holy Spirit.

Jesus Did Not Come to Start a New Religion

Throughout the years, I have come across various definitions of eternal life; all are centered around living forever. However, it is essential to note that everyone will live forever. Whether we spend eternity in heaven or hell is based on our acceptance of Jesus as our Lord. After departing from this earth upon death, we will spend eternity in either of these two places. In John 17:3, Jesus offers us the answer to what eternal life truly means:

> "And this is eternal life, that they may know You, the only true God, and Jesus Christ whom You have sent."

The key to eternal life lies in having a close and intimate relationship with God. This is emphasized by the word *ginosko*, translated as "know" in the verse. It refers to a deep level of understanding. This exact Greek word is also translated as "know" in Mary's response to the angel:

> Then Mary said to the angel, "How can this be, since I do not *know* a man?" (Luke 1:34, emphasis added)

Jesus' purpose was not to establish a new religion through His crucifixion but to restore humanity's relationship with God. Unlike many other religions, this goal cannot be found elsewhere; it is only possible through Christ.

It's essential to recognize that God didn't send Jesus to establish a new religion. He didn't create the denominations that many people associate themselves with, such as Lutheran, Methodist, or Pentecostal. In God's eyes, we are all His children regardless of our titles or affiliations.

My Conversion Experience

I became a Christian in a traditional Pentecostal church. Unfortunately, there was a sense of pride among the members. We believed that God preferred us because we exclusively had the Holy Spirit. As a result, we looked down on Christians who were not part of our group. We had an unspoken agreement that we were superior to others.

Over time, the Holy Spirit has guided me to recognize my past mistakes. It is essential to acknowledge that God is present and active in all churches, regardless of their name or denomination. My previous assumptions were incorrect.

My Experience with the Holy Spirit in a Country Church

After graduating from Bible school in the early 1990s, I was offered a chance to minister in a small country church. Although the church belonged to an unfamiliar denomination, I decided to accept the invitation despite my doubts. I initially believed they were beyond hope, but the Holy Spirit showed me I needed to give them a chance.

When I arrived, the pastor welcomed me, and we chatted before the service began. However, it became clear quite quickly that we shared different beliefs about the Holy Spirit's role in our current time. Despite this, I knew that I had been led by the Spirit to accept the invitation, even though I didn't understand the reason.

I planned to deliver a sermon on faith that would be okay with everyone, but the Holy Spirit had different plans. As the service began, He prompted me to speak about Himself. Although we didn't communicate audibly, He talked to me inwardly as He does with all Christians. In a later chapter, we'll cover how to recognize His voice.

I didn't understand why the Spirit asked me to speak about Him. I believed that the people in the church would not be interested in a message based on signs and wonders. However, the Spirit's response changed my perspective completely. He told me that He wanted me to talk about His identity rather than His actions.

In 1 Corinthians 12:7–11, Paul provides us with a list of the gifts of the Holy Spirit. Typically, before the service in that small country church, these would have been the main focus of my message. However, the Spirit asked me not to focus on what He does. Instead, He prompted me to emphasize that He desires a relationship with us that is not based on what we want to receive from Him.

As I began to address the congregation, I was directed by the Spirit to use Paul's words in 2 Corinthians 13:14 as my text:

> The grace of the Lord Jesus Christ, and the love of God, and the communion of the Holy Spirit be with you all. Amen.

The term *communion* suggests the presence of a connection. As previously stated, Jesus created an opportunity for us to bond with

God through His redemptive work. During my sermon at that rural church, I emphasized the possibility of a relationship with the Holy Spirit that all believers can have.

As I finished my message, I was shocked to see tears streaming down the pastor's face. Despite being new to the ministry, I had anticipated a different reaction. The congregation was equally surprised, and everyone was silent for what felt like an eternity. Finally, the pastor spoke up and asked me to introduce him to the Holy Spirit. He had dedicated years of his life to serving God but had yet to experience a close relationship with his creator.

No One Is Immune from Unbelief

When I began my journey as a Christian, I was part of a group with great pride. We didn't realize that we were just as skeptical as other Christians. It was a revelation to me when I discovered this truth. We considered ourselves "Pentecostal" and believed that the Holy Spirit blessed us above others in the Christian community. However, I am grateful that the Holy Spirit helped me understand the teachings in James 2:14–17:

> What does it profit, my brethren, if someone says he has faith but does not have works? Can faith save him? If a brother or sister is naked and destitute of daily food, and one of you says to them, "Depart in peace, be warmed and filled," but you do not give them the things which are needed for the body, what does it profit? Thus also faith by itself, if it does not have works, is dead.

It is one thing to say you believe in miraculous demonstrations of the Spirit's presence. There are many Christians who profess that they do. Our actions, unfortunately, often tell a different story. We are often steeped in religious tradition, living far below our rights and privileges in Christ.

I want to experience God's plan for my life fully, and I'm sure you do too. This means we must move beyond believing in God and develop a personal relationship with Him. When we approach God from a place of intimacy, it becomes easier to receive from Him.

Thomas Struggled to Believe in the Resurrection

Many people, including the devil, acknowledge the existence of God. However, there is a significant distinction between simply believing in God and having a deep, personal trust in Him. While acknowledging God's existence can be done through natural reasoning, genuinely believing in Him requires a close relationship with Him.

Thomas was a faithful companion of Jesus throughout His ministry. He was present at all gatherings and witnessed every miracle. However, Thomas also had doubts when his fellow disciples informed him of Jesus' resurrection (John 20:26–29). We should avoid rushing to judgment and take the time to reflect on our own faith before criticizing him.

Relationship with God Is Our Foundation

After Jesus appeared to the other disciples, he "breathed" the Holy Spirit into their spirits, which led to their conversion. However, Thomas was not present then and had to rely on his natural reasoning when the other disciples informed him that Jesus had risen from the dead and appeared to them.

It's a simple truth that every person who accepts Jesus as their Lord has the Holy Spirit within them. This Spirit is always available and eager to spend time with us. Sadly, I've met many Christians who are unaware of this truth, each with their own struggles in the Christian journey.

In John 16:7, Jesus informed His disciples that His departure would be beneficial for them. It would open the door for the arrival of the Holy Spirit. We will explore the type of relationship that one can have by seeking Him.

Our Christian faith is built on our connection with God. He sent Jesus to die on the cross as the ultimate payment for our sins. This sacrifice made it possible for us to be made righteous, and God is always ready to welcome us into His presence with open arms.

Chapter 2

Unbelief, Relationship, and the Works of Jesus

> *"Most assuredly, I say to you, he who believes in Me, the works that I do he will do also; and greater works than these he will do, because I go to My Father."*
>
> JOHN 14:12

When Jesus was on earth, He urged His disciples to perform the same works He did, and even greater ones. While many have talked about their ability to do so, we should consider whether we are doing the same works that Jesus did during His time on earth. Personally, I cannot claim to do so, but that should not discourage us from striving toward this achievable goal.

What Is a Belief?

We must comprehend the requirement of belief before we understand why we need to do the "works" that Jesus did. Jesus informed His disciples that those who believed in Him would perform these works (John 14:12). Therefore, if we are not doing the works of Jesus, it implies that we do not have the faith to do so.

I once heard a minister define a *belief* as a firm persuasion based on knowledge. In context, the knowledge he spoke of comes from God's

Word. We talked previously about the difference between acquired and revelation knowledge. Revelation knowledge is required to perform the works of Jesus.

Over the years, the Holy Spirit has broadened my understanding of belief. I now know that it is a strong conviction that stems from the knowledge acquired through one's relationship with God. Fostering a relationship with Him is vitally important.

The Works of Jesus Flow from Our Relationship with Him

When I first became a Christian, I tried to rationalize the miracles that Jesus performed. I constantly devised new justifications for why we weren't seeing them today. However, I came to understand that Jesus' message was simple and straightforward—it all comes down to belief. Without a strong connection to God built through an intimate relationship, we will have difficulty fully accepting this truth.

I believe the main reason for our disbelief is our difficulty understanding that God accepts us. According to Paul, God selected us to be part of His family before He even created the world (Ephesians 1:4). We can only fully enjoy the benefits of being part of God's family through the sacrifice of Jesus.

Do Our Traditions Hinder the Works of Jesus?

Let's take a moment to consider our religious traditions and how they affect our relationship with God. If you are like me, you may not have given much thought to this area. I used to sing with the church worship team without considering the words. One day the Holy Spirit prompted me to look at the overhead slides the church used to project each song's words.

I will use the words from a song by Johnny Cash, often sung in many churches, as an example. It is called "Wayfaring Stranger." The following is a sample of the lyrics:

> I'm just a poor wayfaring stranger
> Traveling through this world below
> There's no sickness, no toil or danger
> In that bright land to which I go

Can you see what is wrong with these lyrics? While it is true that we are traveling through this world, we are not "poor wayfaring strangers." Consider the following scriptures that tell us about our position in Christ:

> Therefore, if anyone is in Christ, he is a new creation; old things have passed away; behold, all things have become new. (2 Corinthians 5:17)

> For He made Him who knew no sin to be sin for us, that we might become the righteousness of God in Him. (2 Corinthians 5:21)

> But you have not so learned Christ, if indeed you have heard Him and have been taught by Him, as the truth is in Jesus: that you put off, concerning your former conduct, the old man which grows corrupt according to the deceitful lusts, and be renewed in the spirit of your mind, and that you put on the new man which was created according to God, in true righteousness and holiness. (Ephesians 4:20–24)

Every Christian is filled with the Spirit of God and can walk in victory over every circumstance. There will be storms along the way, but the Holy Spirit is with us at each step. He wants to help us and will be waiting for any who are willing to spend time with Him each day.

Are We Preaching the Same Message as Jesus and Paul?

I classify the works of Jesus as teaching, preaching, and healing the sick based on the Gospel accounts. Jesus taught more than He preached and preached more than He healed. We have teaching and preaching, but how often do we see miracles manifesting in our midst?

Over the years, I've heard ministers tell their congregations that miracles are no longer needed in the church today. Consider Paul's words in his first letter to the Corinthian Christians:

> And I, brethren, when I came to you, did not come with excellence of speech or of wisdom declaring to you the testimony of God. For I determined not to know anything among you except Jesus Christ and Him crucified. I was with you in weakness, in fear, and in much trembling. And my speech and my preaching were not with persuasive words of human wisdom, but in demonstration of the Spirit and of power, that your faith should not be in the wisdom of men but in the power of God. (1 Corinthians 2:1–5)

Paul was considered an educated man. He had sat under the best teachers of his day and risen to leadership among the Jewish people. It would have been easy for him to lean on his acquired knowledge, yet he chose not to. Paul told the Corinthian believers that he "determined not to know anything... except Jesus Christ." The message he preached drew on revelation knowledge received from the

Holy Spirit. In a later chapter, we will examine how you and I can access this knowledge.

Ministering from Relationship

Paul's ministry flowed out of an intimate relationship with the Holy Spirit. The following scriptures show his dependence on the Spirit:

> As they ministered to the Lord and fasted, *the Holy Spirit said*, "Now separate to Me Barnabas and Saul for the work to which I have called them." Then, having fasted and prayed, and laid hands on them, they sent *them* away. (Acts 13:2–3, emphasis added)

> Now when they had gone through Phrygia and the region of Galatia, *they were forbidden by the Holy Spirit* to preach the word in Asia. After they had come to Mysia, they tried to go into Bithynia, but *the Spirit did not permit them*. (Acts 16:6–7, emphasis added)

> The grace of the Lord Jesus Christ, and the love of God, and the communion of the Holy Spirit *be* with you all. Amen. (2 Corinthians 13:14)

Please spend time looking at the account of Paul's ministry in the book of Acts. You will find many more references to the Holy Spirit. When we combine these with Paul's writings, it becomes clear he depended on the Holy Spirit in his life and ministry.

Demonstrations of the Spirit

You will find many accounts of miraculous demonstrations throughout the Gospels and the book of Acts. Mark tells us Jesus worked with the disciples as they ministered and confirmed their message with "accompanying signs" (Mark 16:20). Jesus describes these signs:

> "And these signs will follow those who believe: In My name they will cast out demons; they will speak with new tongues; they will take up serpents; and if they drink anything deadly, it will by no means hurt them; they will lay hands on the sick, and they will recover." (Mark 16:17–18)

I had several professors in Bible college who claimed we no longer needed the miraculous. They reasoned that the church had grown up. What do you think?

There were always large crowds in Jesus' meetings. Why do you think people were drawn to His meetings? Luke answers this question:

> And He came down with them and stood on a level place with a crowd of His disciples and a great multitude of people from all Judea and Jerusalem, and from the seacoast of Tyre and Sidon, who came to hear Him and be healed of their diseases, as well as those who were tormented with unclean spirits. And they were healed. (Luke 6:17–18)

Over the years, I've talked to many pastors who complain of declining membership. The churches that do seem to be growing seek to make people comfortable using what is commonly called "the seeker-friendly model." In my experience, most churches do not see the signs Jesus spoke of in Mark 16.

What Are the Greater Works?

Today, some ministers say that the "greater works" Jesus spoke of are manifested through radio and television broadcasts. Their rationale is that many more people are being reached through technology today. I struggle with this explanation; I think Jesus was referring to something other than technological advancements.

I praise God for technology. We can reach more people today than ever before. You may agree with those who think that is the "greater work." Regardless of whether or not our advancements are what Jesus spoke of, does that absolve us of responsibility to do the works Jesus did?

If you go back and read through the Gospels, you will find that Matthew, Mark, Luke, and John list three works of Jesus: teaching, preaching, and healing the sick. They do not call these out specifically, but each was present in the Lord's ministry.

Luke told us that the people flocked to Jesus' meetings to "hear" the Word and to be "healed." How many people attend our services today with the same expectation? Instead, the majority attend service each week hoping their pastor is anointed to provide what they need from God. Few seem to have any personal expectation that God will miraculously touch them.

The Holy Spirit Wants to Spend Time with Us

We see in Acts 10:38 that God anointed Jesus, and Jesus then ministered from that anointing. He was the "body of Christ" while ministering. Today, the body consists of all believers. God anoints each with the Holy Spirit.

Paul ended his second letter to the Corinthian believers with encouragement to fellowship with the Holy Spirit (2 Corinthians 13:14). Unfortunately, many Christians have not been taught correctly about the Holy Spirit or His ministry. Sadly, far too many in the church today view Him as nothing more than the power manifesting in our services. He is so much more!

Jesus told His disciples we could "know" the Holy Spirit (John 14:17). The Greek word translated as "know" refers to knowledge gained through personal experience. It is similar to the insight a husband or wife gains through association with their spouse.

You may notice that I keep referencing the relationship available to every Christian with the Holy Spirit. I have found over the years that every struggle I've experienced with understanding the things of the Spirit has been resolved by spending time with Him in fellowship around the Word of God.

The focus of Jesus' final discourse to His disciples is in chapters 14 to 17 of John. I encourage you to spend time reading through these chapters. You will find He focused on the Holy Spirit and the Word with references to the Spirit using masculine pronouns such as "He," "Him," or "His" more than thirty times.

Some of the things in this book may be new to you (as they were to me when I first heard them). The idea that the Holy Spirit desires to spend time with me was very radical. I started by asking Him to reveal Himself to me and then set aside time each day to sit quietly and listen. Over time I noticed specific Scripture passages would come to mind, and I would look them up. The Holy Spirit was communicating to me through these promptings. Our communication has become much more precise over time.

The Holy Spirit does not play favorites. He is waiting on the sidelines for an invitation. We cannot perceive spiritual truth from our natural carnal understanding, which is why Jesus sent Him. You only need to ask the Spirit to reveal Himself and then set aside time to spend with Him. If you do this, He will make Himself known to you and begin to reveal Jesus in ways no human can learn through self-effort.

Chapter 3

Stepping Out in Faith to Do the Works of Jesus

"And I will pray the Father, and He will give you another Helper, that He may abide with you forever—the Spirit of truth, whom the world cannot receive, because it neither sees Him nor knows Him; but you know Him, for He dwells with you and will be in you."

JOHN 14:16–17

We closed the previous chapter by discussing the relationship available to all of us with the Holy Spirit. Jesus told His disciples that they would "know Him." The Greek word translated as "know" is *ginosko*, which refers to intimately knowing a person through personal experience. It is the same word Mary used when she questioned Gabriel about her having a child since she had not "known" a man (Luke 1:34).

Look beyond Your Five Physical Senses

Jesus appeared to His disciples shortly after the resurrection. John tells us that the Lord "breathed on them" and told them to receive the Holy Spirit (John 20:22). The Greek text says that Jesus breathed the Spirit into their spirits. I believe this was the moment they received salvation.

Thomas was not with the disciples when Jesus appeared to them. They told him about their experience with the Lord. He refused to believe without physical evidence to prove that Jesus was alive (John 20:25). Many Christians have Thomas's mentality when it comes to the miraculous power of God. They desire physical proof, but the Bible tells us we are to "walk by faith, not by sight" (2 Corinthians 5:7).

Thomas wanted to see the "print of the nails" and the holes in the Lord's body. He did not understand that even though it was possible to touch Jesus' glorified body, it was still spiritual. It is not possible to perceive something spiritual with our five physical senses. Thomas struggled with this; he was so used to seeing Jesus in His physical body that he could not perceive the truth of the Lord's resurrection.

Lack of awareness of spiritual matters has caused us to believe that what our five physical senses perceive is reality. Society has elevated science as the sole source of truth. The Word of God is truth; science can only reveal natural facts. I believe this is why Paul told the Corinthian believers that the things "seen" are temporary and cannot be depended on (2 Corinthians 4:18).

Jesus told the disciples that signs would follow people who believed the gospel message (Mark 16:17–18). I have found that most people do not view their circumstances through the lens of Scripture. Instead, they lean on things like the traditions taught in their churches, life circumstances, or physical symptoms. If a belief grows out of knowledge gained in our relationship with God and not our physical senses, then our dependence on external situations explains why we struggle with unbelief.

You will find it impossible to break the cycle of unbelief without first developing an intimate relationship with the Word of God and the Holy Spirit. You cannot build intimacy with the Spirit outside of a personal relationship with Scripture. Like any natural relationship, we must commit time to make this happen.

Walking on Water in the Storm

Matthew recounts Peter and Jesus walking on water in the fourteenth chapter of his Gospel (Matthew 14:22–33). Jesus had to compel His disciples to get into the boat. They were professional fishermen who most likely recognized a storm was approaching. It hit so hard that the disciples thought their ship would sink, but then Jesus appeared in the middle of the storm.

All twelve of the men saw Jesus approaching their boat. Only Peter called out to the Lord, asking Him to call him to walk on water. Jesus answered, and Peter stepped out of the boat with the storm raging around him. He successfully walked on water as long as his eyes remained fixed on Jesus.

I believe God is looking for people who will step out of their proverbial boats amid whatever storms are raging in their lives. We must be willing to do so if our goal is to break the aforementioned cycles of unbelief. It will challenge our flesh to do so. There are numerous natural reasons not to step out in faith that we can use as excuses.

Avoiding the Devil's Traps

The Holy Spirit is standing by to help us. If we step out of the boat, we will find Him waiting to empower us to walk above the raging storms. He will empower us to step into the authority available to every Christian in Christ Jesus. You will successfully escape the devil's traps only through this authority.

I will reference religious traditions throughout this book. These are doctrinal truths based on acquired knowledge. Satan uses them to rob Christians of the power available to them through the name of Jesus. I believe that Jesus was referring to acquired knowledge when He said that the traditions of men would render the Word of God powerless (Mark 7:13). God will never reward our self-effort.

Obedience without Question

I once heard a minister say the key to experiencing miracles is to obey God without question. The writer of Hebrews tells us it is impossible to please God outside of faith (Hebrews 11:6). We will never reach the highest levels of faith without first developing a relationship with God.

The Holy Spirit desires to lead us. We must look to Him for guidance in good and bad times. Jesus sent Him to guide us through every storm of life, but He is only able to if we first acknowledge His presence. You can achieve everything God asks of you and receive all Christ has provided by walking in partnership with the Holy Spirit. The only question is whether you will look to Him or choose the path of self-effort.

There are a lot of people who fear stepping out in faith. They fear failure, so they do nothing. The potential for failure will always exist. We are human and cannot escape the fact that all of us, at one time or another, will make mistakes while attempting to follow the Holy Spirit's leading. I have come to a place where I would rather fall flat trying to follow Him than sit on the sidelines doing nothing.

It is still possible to step into the game if you've been sitting on the sidelines. The Holy Spirit is standing by to help you. Just get up, dust yourself off, and step out into God's plan for your life. Ultimately, the only ones who will fail are those who never do anything. So, are you ready to get out of the proverbial boat and face the storms in your life head-on?

Spending Time with the Holy Spirit

There are a lot of Christians who have never grown in their relationship with God. I believe many are like I was in my early years following God. I thought God was angry and ready to judge every mistake because of the teaching I heard. The concept of relationship was foreign to me.

Over time, I've grown to understand how loving our God is. He sent Jesus to die on the cross as payment for our sins before you or I ever committed our first sin. You will always find He is willing to spend time when you approach Him.

Paul tells us that Jesus has made us "accepted" by God (Ephesians 1:6). We approach the Father through the blood of Jesus. Our standing before God, therefore, is based on our position in Christ Jesus.

Spending time and developing a relationship with God may be foreign to you. I began my journey by telling Him what I read in Scripture and about my day. Over time, insights about the verses I was reading started to pop into my mind. Ideas would appear in my mind about the situations I was facing. These are ways the Holy Spirit speaks to us.

The master key to developing a relationship with God is simply starting. Set aside time to talk to Him. He will respond. His response will not be in an audible voice. He speaks to us in a still, small voice that is often like a whisper. At first, it will be challenging to recognize, but it will become much more apparent if you keep spending time with Him.

Growing in Our Relationship with Him

The writer of Hebrews talks about growing up beyond "milk" to the more profound things of God that the Holy Spirit longs to teach us (Hebrews 5:12–13). Unfortunately, failure to recognize His presence has hindered many people from doing this. The root issue is a need for more balanced teaching about the Spirit and His ministry.

Have you ever watched a child learn to walk? They stand, fall, and then do it again. Children do not quit after their first failure. They keep at it until they are walking. Christians should practice the same persistence while developing their relationship with God!

Jesus told us that we would do the same works He did (John 14:12). Doing so requires us to rely on Him wholly. Unfortunately, many ministers do not understand the Holy Spirit and are not teaching people about Him. A lot of the frustration people experience in their Christian walk is due to their need for more understanding in this area.

What Is a Belief?

You may remember the definition of *belief* is a firm persuasion based on knowledge—specifically, the knowledge of Scripture. When I first heard it, this definition resonated in my spirit but left questions in my mind. Many people have knowledge of Scripture but still struggle to believe the promises of God.

The Holy Spirit kept reminding me of the definition for several months. I prayed over it but still could not get settled. I set aside time to listen one day and finally received my answer. It was the word you've seen multiple times: relationship.

So, what is a belief? It is a firm persuasion based on knowledge *gained in a personal relationship*. This knowledge is not acquired through self-effort. You must set aside time each day to read Scripture and talk to the Holy Spirit about what you read to develop the level of belief required to manifest the promises of God.

Mind Renewal

Paul speaks of the renewing of our minds in Romans 12:2:

> And do not be conformed to this world, but be transformed by the renewing of your mind, that you may prove what *is* that good and acceptable and perfect will of God.

Many people struggle with the concept of mind renewal because they lack awareness of the three parts of our being. Paul references each in 1 Thessalonians 5:23:

> Now may the God of peace Himself sanctify you completely; and may your whole spirit, soul, and body be preserved blameless at the coming of our Lord Jesus Christ.

Our spirit is recreated when we make Jesus the Lord of our life. Paul tells us we become new creations in Christ Jesus (2 Corinthians 5:17). Christians refer to this experience as being "born again." It affects our spirit but not our soul or body.

The soul consists of our mind, will, intellect, and emotions. James tells us that our souls are saved through the implanted Word (James 1:21). I believe the process of planting God's Word in our souls is what Paul referenced when he spoke of renewing our minds.

Are You Committed to Him?

Walking by faith requires us to commit ourselves to God's Word. It is the foundation on which we build our relationship with the Holy Spirit. You will find it much easier to discern His leading the more time you spend alone with Him in the Word.

You may have struggled with faith just as I did early in my Christian walk. You will find freedom, like I did, as your focus turns from your efforts to growing faith toward a relationship. The Christian life has become much easier for me to live when I live from a place of intimacy with the Spirit of God.

Jesus told His disciples they could know the Spirit as those outside the church could not (John 14:17). The Spirit entered your spirit when you became a Christian. He is with you at every moment of the day and desires to spend time with you. Like any natural relationship, you must commit time and energy to Him each day. You will find He is more than willing to reciprocate and dedicate time to being with you.

Chapter 4

Natural or Genuine Belief?

*You believe that there is one God. You do well.
Even the demons believe—and tremble!*

JAMES 2:19

I have heard many people talk about believing in God over the years. There is a difference between believing that God exists and believing in Him. James tells us Satan and his minions also believe. They do not have a relationship with God and do not believe in the way we have discussed.

You need to be aware that the world has two types of beliefs. We access the first through acquired knowledge. The second grows out of an intimate relationship with God and His Word; I call this a genuine belief. Some others refer to it as spiritual belief. Jesus referenced this type of belief in Mark 11:23–24:

> "For assuredly, I say to you, whoever says to this mountain, 'Be removed and be cast into the sea,' and does not doubt in his heart, but believes that those things he says will be done, he will have whatever he says. Therefore I say to you, whatever things you ask when you pray, believe that you receive *them,* and you will have *them.*"

I used to struggle with these verses and experienced many faith failures. The Lord placed me under ministers who taught what many refer to as "the faith message." They shared stories of victories achieved in their lives that resulted from having faith as Jesus directed in Mark 11. The stories excited me, but I did not see the same results in my life when I attempted to follow their steps.

Perhaps you have had the same frustrations. The Holy Spirit has helped me understand why I had so much trouble exercising faith to access the provision of God. It all came down to the difference between natural and genuine belief.

Relationship before Faith

Seeing people leave a meeting without receiving what they had hoped for from God has never ceased to bother me. I spent many hours in prayer over this in the early years of my ministry. I had not yet learned that genuine belief grows out of an intimate relationship.

Many people approach God with a plan B in place. I used to do this. You will, too, if you do not step back and focus on developing your relationship before attempting to exercise faith. Thankfully, God is merciful and will work in our lives even when we make mistakes and do not check all the boxes.

People have approached me at the altar for prayer over the years and told me how they had "tried" faith. Most were trying to emulate the steps they saw someone else take. We are called to follow Jesus—not any human being. Doing so is extremely difficult if we do not first develop a relationship and get to know Him.

Natural Belief or Mental Assent?

I have heard people talk about believing God. James tells us Satan also believes in Him (James 2:19). I have mentioned the difference between natural and genuine belief. The Bible describes how the latter flows from the heart:

> For with the heart one believes unto righteousness, and with the mouth confession is made unto salvation. (Romans 10:10)

The Holy Spirit lives in the born again human spirit. He is with you and will help you move from your natural understanding into a genuine belief and unshakable faith.

Some refer to natural belief as mental assent. I agree with this; it describes a condition in which we only agree with Scripture from the soul. Our spirit is not involved. As a result, there is no revelation knowledge on which to stand.

We all desire to see the power of God manifest in our lives. A genuine belief flows from the spirit and is given birth in our relationship with God. It will propel us beyond our natural beliefs and mental assent to God's Word. When this happens, nothing can stop the power of God from manifesting in our lives.

The storms of life will not quickly shake people who have moved from their natural beliefs into genuine ones. They will be firmly fixed on the promises of God and will not need to wonder if they are in faith. Storms will come into their lives, as they do for all, but they will not overcome them.

Thomas's Struggle with Natural Belief

Far too many Christians seem to lean on acquired knowledge. A genuine belief grows out of the heart deeply rooted in the Word of God. The seed from which it springs is revelation knowledge. Many Christians are powerless because they depend on acquired knowledge of Scripture. Thomas is a perfect example of someone who depended on knowledge gained with the physical senses:

> The other disciples therefore said to him, "We have seen the Lord." So he said to them, "Unless I see in His hands the print of the nails, and put my finger into the print of the nails, and put my hand into His side, I will not believe." And after eight days His disciples were again inside, and Thomas with them. Jesus came, the doors being shut, and stood in the midst, and said, "Peace to you!" Then He said to Thomas, "Reach your finger here, and look at My hands; and reach your hand here, and put it into My side. Do not be unbelieving, but believing." And Thomas answered and said to Him, "My Lord and my God!" Jesus said to him, "Thomas, because you have seen Me, you have believed. Blessed are those who have not seen and yet have believed." (John 20:25–29)

Without physical evidence, Thomas could not believe that Jesus had risen from the dead. He was no different than many of us today.

I have prayed with people for healing who were just like Thomas. They could not believe that God had imparted His healing power without some form of physical evidence. God has mercy, and some of these individuals received a miracle, but most walked away without one.

The Provision Has Been Made

Peter tells us that God has already provided everything we will ever need:

> As His divine power has given to us all things that pertain to life and godliness, through the knowledge of Him who called us by glory and virtue. (2 Peter 1:3)

The Word of God reveals His will and plan for our lives. Many people need help to believe in His promises because they are not opening the Bible and spending time meditating on its truths. Meditation is a fancy word used to describe fixed and focused attention. If you commit time each day to fix your attention on Scripture and nothing else, you will plant the seeds from which revelation knowledge will grow.

Jesus went to the cross and died to pay the penalty for our sins. In His sacrifice, provision was made for every need we will experience in our spirits, souls, and bodies. He has completed His work; now it is up to us to believe. God will never force us to receive His blessings. Whether we pursue them or not, He always desires the best for us and will work to ensure we have it.

Are We Living at a Substandard Level of Faith?

Many Christians operate on substandard levels of faith. It is no wonder the power of God is not flowing in more significant measures today! I have heard Christians blame God for their inability to receive what they are seeking from Him. We must accept that the problem is not with Him. He has already provided for every area of our life. As we saw in 2 Peter 1:3, His provision is accessed through His Word.

It is much easier to blame God for our failures in spiritual matters than to accept that we are in a state of unbelief. Consider a situation in which you prayed for someone and they fell over dead. Would you prefer to face their family and say God took them or admit the possibility that you were not developed in faith as you should have been? Doesn't it seem like it would be easier to pin the fault on God? I believe our unwillingness to accept responsibility for our failures is one of the root reasons we do not see more significant manifestations of God's power today.

Revelation Knowledge Is Available to All

Many people in churches today have elevated ministers to an almost godlike level. It is almost as if we think God prefers to impart His revelation knowledge to those with a string of degrees attached to their name. Unfortunately, those with the most degrees teach natural beliefs from the pulpit. Without realizing it, these men and women are essentially teaching God did not mean what He had the Holy Spirit inspire the writers of Scripture to say.

Paul told his readers in Corinth that he had not leaned on "excellence of speech or of wisdom" when he was with them (1 Corinthians 2:1). He understood the difference between acquired and revelation knowledge. The same Holy Spirit that taught Paul is available to guide you today.

You have the Holy Spirit dwelling in your spirit. He is the author of Scripture. There is no requirement for any of us to learn Greek or Hebrew. The Bible's author lives inside us and stands by to teach us. You only have to acknowledge His presence and set aside time to discuss your questions with Him.

So, the Word of God will work for anyone willing to pay the price to meditate on its truths. Once again, meditation is just a fancy term. It means we are committing time to give focused and constant attention to the Word until its truths become revelation knowledge in our spirits. No amount of education is required!

Chapter 5

Why Are We Not Walking in the Power of the Early Church?

And He came down with them and stood on a level place with a crowd of His disciples and a great multitude of people from all Judea and Jerusalem, and from the seacoast of Tyre and Sidon, who came to hear Him and be healed of their diseases, as well as those who were tormented with unclean spirits. And they were healed. And the whole multitude sought to touch Him, for power went out from Him and healed them all.

LUKE 6:17–19

Why do you think people flocked to Jesus' meetings? I do not believe they were there because He was a polished speaker. We have an abundance of eloquent speakers in the church today. If a finely polished sermon was enough, why are we not experiencing more extraordinary measures of God's power today?

Teaching and Discipleship Are Inseparable

Jesus' meetings overflowed with people because of the power He manifested following His teachings. The Gospel accounts and Acts contain many examples of the gospel message being confirmed with miraculous demonstrations of power.

In Matthew 28:19–20, we find what is often called the Great Commission. It begins with the commandment to "go therefore and make disciples of all nations." The Greek word used is *matheteuo*, which is accurately translated as "to teach, instruct" or "to be a disciple of one." It is not possible to separate the concept of discipleship from teaching. We see examples of Jesus' teaching ministry in the following verses:

> And Jesus went about all Galilee, teaching in their synagogues, preaching the gospel of the kingdom, and healing all kinds of sickness and all kinds of disease among the people. (Matthew 4:23)

> Then Jesus went about all the cities and villages, teaching in their synagogues, preaching the gospel of the kingdom, and healing every sickness and every disease among the people. (Matthew 9:35)

> Now it came to pass, when Jesus finished commanding His twelve disciples, that He departed from there to teach and to preach in their cities. (Matthew 11:1)

There are many more verses we could examine. A true disciple of Jesus follows His teachings. To do this, we must be taught. Numerous examples in Scripture show miraculous demonstrations always accompany the gospel message.

Jesus Confirms the Word with Signs

We see in Mark 16:15 that Jesus commissioned His disciples to preach the gospel message. The exciting part of this chapter is found in verses 17–18, where He talks about the signs that will follow those who "believe." If you examine the passage carefully, you'll see that the signs were to follow those who believed the message.

What type of belief is required to see these manifestations Jesus spoke of? It is the genuine belief built in a relationship that we have discussed. The gospel message plants seeds in our souls that grow into this genuine belief.

The Early Church Flowed in the Miraculous

When the early Christians entered a town, the people would know they arrived. They did not have to announce their presence by advertising on billboards, and they did not use social media to draw crowds. The people of one town even referred to Paul as the man who had turned the world upside down (Acts 17:6). In another city, the people marveled at Peter and John:

> Now when they saw the boldness of Peter and John, and perceived that they were uneducated and untrained men, they marveled. And they realized that they had been with Jesus. (Acts 4:13)

The early church operated at a much different ministry level than we do today. Notice that the author of Acts tells us that the people recognized "they had been with Jesus." Peter and John's boldness in ministry was an outgrowth of their relationship with Jesus.

Many churches today have adopted a seeker-friendly model. They aim to create an environment where no visitor would ever feel uncomfortable. These churches often have the largest crowds but rarely experience the miraculous. Our quest to be acceptable has resulted in conformity to the world's methods (Romans 12:2).

Have We Become Indifferent to the Miraculous?

Peter and John were arrested and commanded to no longer preach in the name of Jesus after they healed a lame man at the Beautiful Gate and Peter preached a sermon to the people who had witnessed it. Interestingly, the leaders commanded them to stop teaching but did not command them to stop healing people. Did they see a difference in the authority behind Peter's message and their message?

Peter and John were released and immediately returned to their friends. The group began to pray. I find it interesting that they included a petition to speak the Word of God with boldness after they had been commanded not to speak the name of Jesus:

> "Now, Lord, look on their threats, and grant to Your servants that with all boldness they may speak Your word, by stretching out Your hand to heal, and that signs and wonders may be done through the name of Your holy Servant Jesus." (Acts 4:29–30)

Today, men and women fill pulpits, preaching the wisdom of men. They use eloquent words, and some even preach messages they receive through subscription services. Paul described our current situation in his second letter to Timothy:

> For the time will come when they will not endure sound doctrine, but according to their own desires, *because* they have itching ears, they will heap up for themselves teachers; and they will turn *their* ears away from the truth, and be turned aside to fables. (2 Timothy 4:3–4)

The Jewish leaders recognized that Peter and John were uneducated and untrained (Acts 4:13). They could not explain the miraculous healing of the lame man. Peter and John's prayer in Acts 4 shows a complete dependence on God that overrode their lack of formal education. What would happen today if we prayed from the same place in our relationship with God?

The First Use of the Term *Christian*

The term *Christian* was first applied to the followers of Jesus in Antioch:

> And when he had found him, he brought him to Antioch. So it was that for a whole year they assembled with the church and taught a great many people. And the disciples were first called Christians in Antioch. (Acts 11:26)

The disciples spent a year teaching the people in Antioch. It was during this time that the term originated. Initially, it was meant to be a derogatory term. The church embraced it, and we still use it to describe ourselves today.

Christian was coined to describe those who walked as Jesus walked and did the same works He did. The people of Antioch used it because Paul, Barnabas, and the other Christians acted as Jesus had when He ministered on the earth. How many people who have interacted with you have accused you of acting like Jesus?

Following the Example of Jesus

Paul encouraged the Christians in Corinth to follow his example in how he pursued Jesus (1 Corinthians 11:1). God expects us to follow the example of Jesus in our lives and ministries. The Gospel accounts show us how Jesus operated and ministered.

One glaring detail that stands out in Jesus' and the early church's ministries is that they did not sit around praying for the Spirit of

God to move. They walked in the anointing and power of the Spirit. Revival followed them in every place they visited. We see this in the prayer offered when John and Peter were released and the church gathered to pray (Acts 4:29–30). They petitioned for boldness, expecting Jesus to confirm the Word they ministered with miraculous signs.

Paul Expected the Miraculous to Follow His Messages

Peter and John were unlearned and untrained but still saw the miraculous following their ministries. Paul was different. Some of the most outstanding teachers of his day had taught him while he was growing up. If anyone could put together a polished sermon, it would have been him. Notice what he wrote about the message he preached in his letter to the Corinthian Christians:

> And my speech and my preaching were not with persuasive words of human wisdom, but in demonstration of the Spirit and of power, that your faith should not be in the wisdom of men but in the power of God. (1 Corinthians 2:4–5)

A lot of men and women standing in pulpits today use "persuasive words of human wisdom" they learned in seminary. Paul's ministry was followed by demonstrations "of the Spirit and of power." I believe the Lord worked with Paul and confirmed the gospel message he preached (Mark 16:20).

Some claim the need for miraculous signs and wonders has passed. What do you think? From what we've seen in this chapter, don't they exist to confirm God's Word? If that is true, wouldn't the argument they are no longer needed also mean the Word is no longer needed? I think the answer is clear. Do you agree?

Chapter 6

Have We Become Complacent?

*"So shall My word be that goes forth from My mouth;
It shall not return to Me void,
But it shall accomplish what I please,
And it shall prosper in the thing for which I sent it."*

ISAIAH 55:11

I often wonder if Christians have unknowingly allowed themselves to become overly comfortable with the state of things. In *The Pursuit of God: The Human Thirst for the Divine*, A. W. Tozer wrote, "Complacency is a deadly foe of all spiritual growth." Is it possible we've become complacent by pursuing church models meant to make the "seeker" comfortable?

Contending for the Faith

Many Christians that I have interacted with over the years seem to be content with the current state of the church. They are not pressing into the things of God. Sadly, the majority would be unwilling to welcome the Holy Spirit into service for fear of Him doing something that would make people uncomfortable.

I have recently spoken of a relationship as the goal of our salvation. God sent Jesus to open the door for humanity to be restored to fellowship with Him. Our relationship with God must be nurtured and nourished each day, or it will begin to wither. Many have started on fire for God only to become comfortable with their Christianity and stop pursuing Him. Complacency is far too common in our churches today.

Jude speaks of the need for diligence in our pursuit of the things of God:

> Beloved, while I was very diligent to write to you concerning our common salvation, I found it necessary to write to you exhorting you to contend earnestly for the faith which was once for all delivered to the saints. (Jude 1:3)

Jude speaks of contending "earnestly for the faith." The devil will not make it easy for us to do this. We must be willing to fight if our goal is to emerge victorious and receive the full manifestation of God's power.

Are We Walking in the Same Faith as the Early Church?

The faith operating in most of our lives is not like that of the early Christians. Some will argue otherwise. Think about the miraculous manifestations we spoke about in the previous chapter. If we walk in the same faith, why don't we see the same results?

Peter tells us we have "like precious faith" as he and the other apostles had (2 Peter 1:1). Paul tells us God has given us "a measure of faith" (Romans 12:3), which I believe is the same faith Peter wrote about. We have the same faith that Jesus, the apostles, and the early church walked in. Unfortunately, our reliance on acquired knowledge has resulted in us leaning more on our natural faith than the faith God provides in our spirits.

Over the years, I've heard so-called "prophets" deliver "words" from God. They claim God says He is sending a mighty move of the Spirit that will shake the nations. I've always wanted to ask the men and women who utter these words if God expects anything from us. They imply He will do it while we sit back and watch.

These so-called "words from God" enable complacency. Why would we need to contend for the faith if God will do all the work for us? I think there is at times a mindset permeating the church that places the blame for our lack of power on God rather than accepting responsibility ourselves.

The Holy Spirit spoke to me about these things recently. He told me that the world is waiting on an outflowing of His power while we hide in our prayer closets, calling for God to pour it out. Consider the words of Paul in the following verses:

> But even if our gospel is veiled, it is veiled to those who are perishing, whose minds the god of this age has blinded, who do not believe, lest the light of the gospel of the glory of Christ, who is the image of God, should shine on them. (2 Corinthians 4:3–4)

Every Christian is called to the ministry of reconciliation. We are to proclaim the Word of God to the dark world around us. The Lord works with us and confirms His Word just as He did with the apostles and early Christians (Mark 16:20). This is only true if we are actively working on our relationship with Him and giving constant and continuous attention to His Word.

A Living Relationship with God

Christianity is meant to be a living relationship between us and our creator. The reaction I receive from most Christians when they hear me say this saddens me. Few seem to understand that the Holy Spirit is with them and desires to spend time with them daily. As I mentioned earlier, relationships must be nurtured and nourished to last.

Many people are more concerned with what their friends or church members think of them than with what God thinks. Walking in the miraculous will require us to fear God more than man. Our reliance on man's opinion is one way complacency manifests in the church today.

Persecution Follows the Power

Paul and his companions were not always well received:

> Now it happened in Iconium that they went together to the synagogue of the Jews, and so spoke that a great multitude both of the Jews and of the Greeks believed. But the unbelieving Jews stirred up the Gentiles and poisoned their minds against the brethren. Therefore they stayed there a long time, speaking boldly in the Lord, who was bearing witness to the word of His grace, granting signs and wonders to be done by their hands. But the multitude of the city was divided: part sided with the Jews, and part with the apostles. And when a violent attempt was made by both the Gentiles and Jews, with their rulers, to abuse and stone them, they became aware of it and fled to Lystra and Derbe, cities of Lycaonia, and to the surrounding region. And they were preaching the gospel there. (Acts 14:1–7)

The Jewish people in Iconium did not receive Paul's ministry. They even stirred up Gentiles in the area by poisoning their minds against the gospel message Paul preached. The situation reminds me of Paul's words in Colossians 2:8, where he warned his readers about allowing other people's words to derail their Christian walk:

> Beware lest anyone cheat you through philosophy and empty deceit, according to the tradition of men, according to the basic principles of the world, and not according to Christ.

The Greek word translated as "cheat" in this verse paints a picture of a predator carrying off its prey. The enemy uses words, such as those spoken by the Jews in Iconium, to keep the Word of God from being sown. This blocked Paul from preaching the gospel, and we should not be surprised when the same thing happens to us today.

The Paradox in Jesus' Message

We see in passages such as John 7:43 that Jesus' ministry caused divisions. As we saw with Paul in Iconium, ministers who flow in the power of the Spirit should expect persecution. Unfortunately, many have allowed themselves to compromise the message in their pursuit of being accepted by the world around them. The majority do this ignorantly. Regardless of the motivation, the result will always be complacency for those pursuing man's approval above God's.

Jesus' ministry caused division. Demonstrations of miraculous power also followed it. The Holy Spirit always confirmed His preaching. Jesus has called us to follow His example. We must never allow any fear of people's reactions to enter our lives. Consider Jesus' words in the following verses:

> "Therefore whoever confesses Me before men, him I will also confess before My Father who is in heaven. But whoever denies Me before men, him I will also deny before My Father who is in heaven." (Matthew 10:32–33)

> "Peace I leave with you, My peace I give to you; not as the world gives do I give to you. Let not your heart be troubled, neither let it be afraid." (John 14:27)

Is there a paradox in Jesus' message? Publicly He talked of division; then, in private conversations with the disciples, He spoke of peace. There is no conflict in His statements though. He placed His peace in our hearts and will sustain us through the opposition that may result from our obedience to His call.

Peace with God or Man?

John records Jesus' last prayer for the disciples. In His prayer, Jesus warned that the world would not accept us because of our relationship with Him:

> "I have given them Your word; and the world has hated them because they are not of the world, just as I am not of the world." (John 17:14)

We have peace with God because of Jesus Christ (Romans 5:1). God accepts us (Ephesians 1:6), so why should it matter if people accept our ministry? A revelation of these truths is your defense against the temptation to pursue approval from people instead of God. It will also protect us against slipping into a complacent lifestyle void of God's power.

There is no way to deny that the message of the cross is divisive. Many of our churches have compromised by using seeker-friendly models designed to gain acceptance from the unsaved. Most pastors in these churches do not even realize that they have fallen into the enemy's trap and feel they are doing the Lord's works. Revival will not be seen by those who are not willing to confront sin or cause division if necessary.

Persecution and the Godly Lifestyle

Both Jesus and Paul warned that persecution would accompany a godly lifestyle. Very few Christians in Western nations have suffered persecution at the level experienced by the early church. We have become complacent, resulting in a state of ungodliness that is often not recognized within our ranks.

I have heard older ministers warn younger against the danger of offending the people they minister to. Most have the best intentions in doing so. They do not realize their advice contradicts scriptures like those examined in this chapter. We must not forget verses such as 2 Corinthians 6:14 when tempted to make our messages more acceptable to society:

> Do not be unequally yoked together with unbelievers. For what fellowship has righteousness with lawlessness? And what communion has light with darkness?

Acceptance by the world leads to an unequal yoking between light and darkness. Making people comfortable in service and walking in line with Scripture is impossible. We must choose one path or the other. Jesus was not afraid to confront those He ministered to, nor should we be!

One of the greatest enemies in our Christian walk is complacency. Far too many of us have allowed ourselves to become content with how things are going in our churches today. Jesus sent the Holy Spirit to provide fellowship and to empower the church. We cannot begin to fathom how grieved He must be by our pursuit of acceptance and unwillingness to confront sin.

Chapter 7

Believe God's Word or Religious Tradition

"Making the word of God of no effect through your tradition which you have handed down. And many such things you do."

MARK 7:13

We have been discussing the danger of allowing ourselves to become complacent. One cause of complacency is our traditions that develop over time. Most who fall into the trap of "religious tradition" do not even realize they have done so. Satan has snared them into his trap without their knowledge.

Religious Traditions

Organized religion has led many well-meaning Christians into the bondage of its traditions. These traditions are a barrier to seeing God confirm His Word with miraculous demonstrations of power.

I once served as a local pastor for what some would call a traditional denomination. The congregation recited the Apostles' Creed in every service. One of the elders would lead this. They asked if I would allow them to continue with their practice, and my answer caused a division that eventually resulted in my removal as pastor by the local district. What did I say that caused such a stir? I did not want them to recite it out of ritual, but only when the Holy Spirit prompted them to.

Few realize the damage that religious tradition has done to the church. Every church I've been involved with has had some form of this damage. Pentecostal churches have just as many traditions they hold dear as traditional denominations, such as Baptist or Lutheran.

The Label of Our Church Does Not Matter

A lot of people are talking about revival these days. Unfortunately, the church is steeped in religious traditions that have robbed her of the power early Christians walked in. Revival will not come until we turn away from our traditions and make the Word of God first in our lives.

It is time to cast off the mantle of religion and turn back to the Bible. Nothing else will open the door to revival that so many are praying for. We can continue to fast, pray, and cry out to God, but our efforts will not produce results until we put God's Word first.

I have been involved with many churches that fall under the label "charismatic." All seemed to falsely believe they were immune to religious traditions. Every church has traditions that we must be willing to challenge with Scripture. The label on the sign or denomination a church belongs to does not make a difference.

Empty Buildings and Religious Traditions

We have built massive edifices and called them churches. Europe is famous for its cathedrals, such as Notre Dame or St. Peter's Basilica. Weekly services are full of pomp and pageantry. Priests dress in traditional robes and administer sacraments according to denominational practices.

Most church buildings and cathedrals have become nothing more than temples where people gather to worship religious traditions. Very few have any manifestation of God's miraculous power. Jesus did not work with the disciples and confirm their religious practices. He confirmed His Word they preached (Mark 16:20).

People attend service or mass more out of fear than out of love for God. They are terrified they will lose their salvation if they don't partake of the sacraments. I have met many people who profess to be Christians but have no relationship with God. Satan holds them in bondages that only the pure Word of God can break.

Adherence to religious rituals will not grant us an audience with God. Christianity is not about what we do to earn acceptance with Him. Jesus came to fulfill the Law and deliver humanity from its shackles. We have replaced it with our religious traditions.

Several of my Bible college professors told us that people would flock to the meetings of those who preached the "true gospel." Over time I've seen that this is just not true. The Gospel accounts recorded by Matthew, Mark, Luke, and John show it was not just Jesus' messages that drew multitudes to His meetings. The people came because of the miraculous demonstrations of power the Holy Spirit used to confirm Jesus' teachings.

People are no different today than they were when Jesus walked the earth. We all have a hunger for the miraculous. Unfortunately, religious traditions have robbed us of the reality available in Christ, just as Jesus warned they would (Mark 7:13).

Thomas Could Not See Beyond His Natural Understanding

Our hunger will not be satisfied outside of obedience to God's Word. His Word is the sole foundation of our relationship with Him.

Situations or people around us will not influence us when we are walking in step with the Holy Spirit. He will lead us, and it will become easy to identify traditions in our lives that render the Word powerless.

Many people in the church today allow the storms of life to have more influence over them than God's Word. Denominational beliefs that contradict Scripture are often held dear. Some would fight for them even if it meant doing so would cause them to fight Scripture. A conversation between Thomas and Jesus illustrates such a mindset:

> "Let not your heart be troubled; you believe in God, believe also in Me. In My Father's house are many mansions; if *it were* not *so,* I would have told you. I go to prepare a place for you. And if I go and prepare a place for you, I will come again and receive you to Myself; that where I am, *there* you may be also. And where I go you know, and the way you know." Thomas said to Him, "Lord, we do not know where You are going, and how can we know the way?" Jesus said to him, "I am the way, the truth, and the life. No one comes to the Father except through Me." (John 14:1–6)

Thomas interjected reasoning into his interpretation of Jesus' statement. He understood what Jesus said but could not comprehend it with his mind. Jesus told the disciples they would know "the way" to where He was going. Thomas did not believe this. He tried to understand a spiritual truth with his natural mind and failed.

The Word contains spiritual truth that we cannot understand naturally. We will respond to Scripture like Thomas responded to Jesus if our foundation is acquired knowledge only. The spiritual created everything we perceive with our five physical senses and is much more real than anything in the natural realm.

Choosing the Word over Physical Symptoms

Let me use the area of physical healing to illustrate. Peter tells us that Jesus "bore our sins in His own body" and that by Jesus' stripes we were "healed" (1 Peter 2:24). He wrote those statements in the past tense, indicating that Jesus provided healing for our physical bodies in His redemptive work.

Consider Peter's statement. Would you be willing to accept it as truth even if your body is full of symptoms that say it is untrue? Most Christians would choose the input of their physical senses as truth. Without realizing it, we would be choosing to follow Thomas's example.

Many denominations today no longer believe healing is available to us. Some have even inserted this into their official doctrinal statements. The belief that God no longer heals is a tradition that has robbed millions of the blessings available to them through Christ's broken body.

Salvation Is a Spiritual Experience

Walking in the supernatural requires us to firmly decide to look beyond our natural senses. Doing so will put us on the path of our heavenly Father, who Paul tells us "calls those things which do not exist as though they did" (Romans 4:17).

You may question the thought of describing something you cannot see as if it has already manifested. Doing so does not mean we are denying that physical things exist. Let's use salvation to illustrate how we do this. Romans 10:10 says:

> For with the heart one believes unto righteousness, and with the mouth confession is made unto salvation.

Remember when you received Jesus as your Lord and became a Christian? Did you have any corresponding evidence from your five physical senses that validated the experience?

Everything we receive from God flows from the spiritual realm into the natural. There will be no evidence discernable to our feelings; this is where faith comes in. Receiving God's provision requires us to believe before the answer manifests in the natural realm.

Many traditions we hold dear came from natural experiences that countered God's Word. A minister may have prayed for someone who failed to receive healing and even died. Rather than admitting he did not understand, the minister might have chosen to tell the family that person's death was God's will. Over time, people embraced this as truth and no longer believe it is God's will to heal.

God's Word Is Our Sole Source of Truth

Everything we receive from God requires us to believe before the answer is evident in our feelings. Revival is no different. The Holy Spirit enters the human spirit and takes up residence at the moment of conversion. We must acknowledge His presence, move beyond our traditions, and act the way people anointed by the Spirit should.

Our feelings cannot communicate truth. They will provide us with facts that we may need to act on, but facts are not truth. For a Christian, the Word is our sole source of truth. Jesus sent the Holy Spirit to teach and guide us into all truth (John 16:13–15).

I once heard testimony from the Hebrides Revival of 1949 to 1953 that illustrates the point I'm trying to make. The Spirit led people to preach in a village that was unreachable due to flooding. A river stood between them and the town, but water levels were too high to cross. It would have been easy to turn around and wait another day to obey God's direction. Because they had a word from God, they did not allow the flood to hinder them. They walked into the floodwaters, sank to their ankles but no deeper, and then walked across the river! Would we have had the boldness to put our lives at risk as they did?

The wisdom of the world cannot compare to God's wisdom. Paul tells us that God has "made foolish the wisdom of this world" (1 Corinthians 1:20). You will never operate in God's faith if you insist on following your wisdom based on religious tradition, physical senses, or feelings.

Chapter 8

Turn Your Eyes to the Spiritual Realm and Victory Will Follow

And do not be conformed to this world, but be transformed by the renewing of your mind, that you may prove what is that good and acceptable and perfect will of God.

ROMANS 12:2

We must renew our minds and break down our reliance on the natural realm to operate in God's faith. Our five physical senses will hold us captive to the sense realm until we commit to doing whatever it takes to break free from them. It is at this point we will be able to share Paul's testimony in Galatians 1:11–12:

> But I make known to you, brethren, that the gospel which was preached by me is not according to man. For I neither received it from man, nor was I taught *it*, but *it came* through the revelation of Jesus Christ.

Moving beyond Acquired Knowledge

We have spoken of the difference between acquired and revelation knowledge. I have been to Bible college and am not against education.

Unfortunately, our educational institutions have been infused with religious tradition and have produced far too many ministers who have yet to learn revelation knowledge.

Paul was highly educated but recognized the need to move beyond his acquired knowledge. Overall, it seems we've become far too educated to take God at His Word. Our reliance on natural sources of knowledge has resulted in fewer miraculous signs and great manifestations today.

Walking in the Spirit requires a willingness to step out and do things that may look foolish to those limited in understanding. You cannot walk by faith and rely on your natural understanding. Jesus spat on a man's tongue, and a miracle manifested (Mark 7:33). Would you be willing to do something like this if prompted by the Spirit?

Looking into the Spiritual Realm for the Answer

Walking in the power of God will require you to commit to putting the spiritual realm above the natural. Consider the following exchange between Jesus and Thomas:

> "And where I go you know, and the way you know." Thomas said to Him, "Lord, we do not know where You are going, and how can we know the way?" Jesus said to him, "I am the way, the truth, and the life. No one comes to the Father except through Me." (John 14:4–6)

Thomas had a natural relationship with Jesus. He was not born again and could not know Him spiritually. He did not have revelation knowledge of Jesus' divinity and struggled to understand the Lord's words.

Many of us are following the path of Thomas without realizing it. The only foundation for our faith is what we perceive of God by our five physical senses. We need a revelation that God has already moved on our behalf to supply every need through the death, burial, and resurrection of Jesus.

Elisha and the Army of Syria

Elisha and his servant woke one day to find the city where they were staying surrounded by the army of Syria. God had been revealing the battle plans of the Syrian king to Elisha, who then shared them with the king of Israel.

> And when the servant of the man of God arose early and went out, there was an army, surrounding the city with horses and chariots. And his servant said to him, "Alas, my master! What shall we do?" So he answered, "Do not fear, for those who *are* with us *are* more than those who *are* with them." And Elisha prayed, and said, "LORD, I pray, open his eyes that he may see." Then the LORD opened the eyes of the young man, and he saw. And behold, the mountain *was* full of horses and chariots of fire all around Elisha. (2 Kings 6:15–17)

Consider Elisha's response to his servant in the context of our discussion. He was not afraid of the Syrian army; Elisha had a relationship with God and trusted that he and his servant would be protected.

Elisha was looking inward and trusted in God. There is no indication he saw the angelic army that was with him. He just knew it was with him and asked the Lord to open the spiritual eyes of his servant. God answered, and the servant could see the angelic army protecting them.

Later in 2 Kings, we learn that the Lord blinded the eyes of the Syrian soldiers. Elisha led them to the Israeli king, who placed them under guard. Two men overcame the armies of Syria by simply putting their trust in God instead of their five physical senses!

There are many examples of scriptural promises, such as Psalm 91, where God's protection is promised. The qualifier is that we must dwell in relationship with God (Psalm 91:1). I believe that is the place Elisha operated from. His servant, on the other hand, did not.

The servant reminds me of many Christians I've met over the years. He allowed himself to be moved by the input of his five physical senses, which opened the door to fear. Many Christians receive a negative report from the doctor or a late payment notice from a creditor and react like the servant.

From a natural perspective, it isn't easy to trust someone to come through for us if we do not know them. Having secondhand knowledge that they have promised to protect us will not produce confidence. It is no different in the spiritual realm. Faith in God's provision comes only from times of fellowship.

Train Yourself to Look Inward

I have found it much easier to rationalize my situation than look to God for provision. Walking in His promises requires us to open His Word to discover them. Our ignorance of these promises leads us to rationalize why things are happening to us.

If you receive a diagnosis from the doctor that offers little-to-no hope, how would you react? The answer depends on you. Have you been spending time each day with the Holy Spirit, focusing on Scripture, or have you allowed yourself to be distracted by the affairs of life?

If you are focused on something other than the Holy Spirit and God's Word, you will react to situations like a negative diagnosis with your natural reasoning. Most will even begin to rationalize their situations; some will argue their illness is God's will or that He may be trying to teach them something.

Rationalizing our situation means we are making excuses. The bottom line usually is that we have not prioritized our relationship with God. Therefore, we have neglected His Word and cannot release His power into our situations.

We will see in later chapters that Jesus compared the Word to a seed. With any natural seed, you can only expect a harvest if something is planted in the ground. For a Christian, you can walk in victory over any situation, but you must first plant the seed of God's Word in your soul. The process of planting is what Paul describes as mind renewal in Romans 12:2.

Chapter 9

Meditation on God's Word Will Deepen Your Relationship with Him

Let no one despise your youth, but be an example to the believers in word, in conduct, in love, in spirit, in faith, in purity. Till I come, give attention to reading, to exhortation, to doctrine. Do not neglect the gift that is in you, which was given to you by prophecy with the laying on of the hands of the eldership. Meditate on these things; give yourself entirely to them, that your progress may be evident to all. Take heed to yourself and to the doctrine. Continue in them, for in doing this you will save both yourself and those who hear you.

1 TIMOTHY 4:12–16

We have been discussing the need to put God's Word first. Paul told Timothy to give himself to meditation on the Word of God. Meditation is a big word used to describe a time of constant and continuous focus on a particular subject. In this case, we are talking about Scripture.

Paul told Timothy that his sole focus on Scripture would be visible to everyone around him. His statement reminds me of God's instruction to Joshua as he stepped into Moses's shoes to lead Israel:

"This Book of the Law shall not depart from your mouth, but you shall meditate in it day and night, that you may observe to do according to all that is written in it. For then you will make your way prosperous, and then you will have good success." (Joshua 1:8)

Success for the Christian is directly connected to the time we meditate on Scripture. God even appears to have placed responsibility for Joshua's success in leading the nation of Israel on it.

The Cure for Worry and Anxiety

Many Christians suffer from worry and anxiety. Jesus addressed both in Matthew 6:31–34:

> "Therefore do not worry, saying, 'What shall we eat?' or 'What shall we drink?' or 'What shall we wear?' For after all these things the Gentiles seek. For your heavenly Father knows that you need all these things. But seek first the kingdom of God and His righteousness, and all these things shall be added to you. Therefore do not worry about tomorrow, for tomorrow will worry about its own things. Sufficient for the day *is* its own trouble."

A lack of trust causes people to waver in their faith. Christians struggle with worry and anxiety because they lack confidence that God will care for them. Let's revisit the concept of relationship. Can you imagine trusting someone you have never spent time with?

Jesus defined eternal life as knowing God (John 17:3). God desires to spend time with us. He will meet you if you commit to spend time with Him each day. You will find it much easier to walk in faith as you spend more time fellowshipping with God.

A Revelation of Your Identity in Christ Jesus

A person with a clear revelation of their position in Christ will be fearless. Paul's letters provide us with many references to help develop our confidence in God. I recommend starting in the book of Romans and then going through each of Paul's letters to identify these references. Write them out in the first person and spend time each day reviewing them. It is beneficial to read them out loud. Consider the following examples from Ephesians 1 to help you get started:

> "I have been blessed with every spiritual blessing in heavenly places in Christ." (v. 3)

> "I was chosen by God in Christ before the foundation of the world to stand holy and without blame before Him." (v. 4)

> "I was predestined to adoption by Jesus Christ to Himself, according to the good pleasure of His will." (v. 5)

> "In the glory of God's grace I have been made accepted in Christ." (v. 6)

> "In Christ, I have redemption through His blood." (v. 7)

These are just a few examples. If you use them as a guide and continue through just the book of Ephesians, you will have a strong foundation for understanding your identity in Christ.

Confidence Birthed in Relationship with God

I once heard a minister define *belief* as confidence birthed in a relationship. Our faith in a person increases with time as we observe their actions and commitment to do what they say. As we spend time with God daily, our confidence in Him will increase.

As you can tell, the concept of relationship is critical to our discussion in this book. The more time we spend meditating on the Word and discussing what we read with the Holy Spirit, the more our faith in God will increase. It is no different from what happens in a relationship with another person. Our trust in them grows or decreases as we spend more time observing their integrity.

I used to struggle with James 2:14–26, where we read that faith without works is dead. God does not move in response to what we do for Him, so how could faith be dependent on our works? The Holy Spirit has helped me view James' statement in a different light. It could more accurately read, "Faith without trust is dead."

To illustrate my point, let's consider the concept of tithing, an area many people struggle with. Does God base His willingness to bless us on whether or not we tithe? No, He has already blessed us in Christ Jesus, so receiving His financial blessing does not depend on whether or not we give. We give, therefore, when prompted to do so by the Spirit because we trust Him to provide for our needs.

Fellowshipping with the Holy Spirit

Paul closed his second letter to the Corinthian believers with encouragement to commune with the Holy Spirit (2 Corinthians 13:14). The Holy Spirit is the third person of the divine Trinity. He is God, just as Jesus and the Father are also God. When you develop a relationship with the Spirit, you develop a relationship with God.

Many people in the church today seem to have no revelation regarding the Holy Spirit. We teach about Him out of acquired knowledge, but how many ministers have experienced intimacy with the Spirit? I've met very few who have.

More than thirty references to the Holy Spirit use masculine pronouns in chapters 14 to 16 of John. The following verses are two examples:

> "And I will pray the Father, and He will give you another Helper, that *He* may abide with you forever—the Spirit of truth, whom the world cannot receive, because it neither sees *Him* nor knows *Him*; but you know *Him*, for *He* dwells with you and will be in you." (John 14:16–17, emphasis added)

> "However, when *He*, the Spirit of truth, has come, *He* will guide you into all truth; for *He* will not speak on *His* own *authority*, but whatever *He* hears *He* will speak; and *He* will tell you things to come. *He* will glorify Me, for *He* will take of what is Mine and declare *it* to you. All things that the Father has are Mine. Therefore I said that *He* will take of Mine and declare *it* to you." (John 16:13–15, emphasis added)

Jesus sent the Holy Spirit to teach us. He desires to spend time with us each day. I have found that our intimacy with the Spirit is a direct reflection of our intimacy with the Word of God. Many people have attempted to chase spiritual things separate from the Word, and all end up in error.

Perfect Love

John tells us that "perfect love casts out fear" (1 John 4:18). You will find your fears lessen the more you spend time with God and His Word. Freedom from fear is a natural extension of entering into a deeper relationship with God. You will find it challenging to hold on to fear as your relationship with God becomes more intimate.

Fear exists where there is an absence of love. We will experience no anxiety while spending time with the Holy Spirit. He will lead us into a deeper level of intimacy with God. Our fear will diminish as we follow Him daily.

Doubt and unbelief are both rooted in fear. I've said previously that a belief is rooted in a relationship with God. Fear and anxiety are no different. Both are rooted in unbelief. The more we allow ourselves to become intimately involved with things that do not glorify God, the more fear will influence our lives.

Fellowship Is the Answer

James tells us we should have an unwavering faith in God when making petitions (James 1:6). Fear is the root of wavering faith. As mentioned earlier, faith cannot exist without trust. Trust is earned gradually as we spend time with a person. For this reason, the cure for wavering faith is to spend time daily in fellowship with the Holy Spirit and the Word of God. You will find your confidence increasing and you will struggle less to believe God's promises if you commit to doing this.

Our relationship with God is the answer to every problem and struggle. He is waiting with arms wide open to receive us but will not force Himself into our lives. Many ministers today teach formulas and twelve-step lists. Instead, our focus should be on leading those God has called us to minister to into a relationship with Him.

Sadly, most Christians seem more established in acquired knowledge of the world around them than in Scripture. For this reason, they live in an almost endless loop, moving from one tragedy to another. The cure is meditation on Scripture and time spent fellowshipping with the Holy Spirit.

Developing a Relationship with God through Meditation

There are many ways to develop your relationship with God. The most critical way is to meditate on His written Word. You must commit time each day to growing in this discipline if your goal is intimacy with God.

I have found that many Christians only look to God when they have a dire need. It is almost as if we view Him as an ambulance service on standby should an emergency occur. He desires to be involved in every area of our lives but will not force Himself into them.

Meditation on God's Word is the only sure path to victory. The church needs more good teaching on how to meditate. Some resist the concept because they feel it belongs only in ungodly metaphysical religions. They do not realize meditation is much more than clearing their minds and chanting "Om!"

In the simplest of terms, meditation is the practice of giving focused and consistent attention to a specific subject. We practice it while watching television programs, newscasts, movies, or sporting events. Students are meditating on their course materials while studying for exams. Meditation is already a part of our daily life. We need to focus on God and His Word instead of the worldly things around us.

We will find it less and less of a struggle to believe the promises of God if we commit time to developing our relationship with Him. Our trust in Him will increase, enabling us to walk in higher levels of faith. The sad truth, though, is most Christians are more committed to spending time with their televisions and social media accounts than they are to spending time with the Lord. The Holy Spirit is available to guide you in this journey. You will find Him waiting when you shut these things off and ask for His help.

Chapter 10

Making the Word of God the Focus of Your Meditation

Meditate on these things; give yourself entirely to them, that your progress may be evident to all.

1 TIMOTHY 4:15

Paul's letter to Timothy provides a dictionary definition of meditation, which involves giving oneself entirely to God and constantly focusing on Scripture. This discipline is crucial in the Christian life, but unfortunately, many Christians do not fully comprehend its value in strengthening their relationship with God, as discussed in the previous chapter.

What Is Meditation?

Some Christians do not include meditation in their religious practice because they associate it with Eastern or cultic religions. However, it is unnecessary to perform yoga or open our minds to demonic realms to practice meditation.

Do you know what meditation is? According to the dictionary, it's contemplating or reflecting on something. You can meditate on anything, even something as mundane as your grocery list. Sometimes we meditate without realizing it, like when we watch a sitcom, sporting event, or movie.

Paul directed Timothy to meditate on the things he had written to him. He wanted him to keep the truths of God at the forefront of his mind. Notice that Paul even told Timothy that his progress in spiritual matters would be evident to all around him if he did this. Do you think meditating on Scripture would have the same impact on us today?

God Told Joshua Meditation Would Be His Key to Success

God called Joshua to step into Moses's shoes and lead Israel into the Promised Land. We see in the following verse that God even placed the responsibility for success in this task on Joshua:

> "This Book of the Law shall not depart from your mouth, but you shall meditate in it day and night, that you may observe to do according to all that is written in it. For then you will make your way prosperous, and then you will have good success." (Joshua 1:8)

For Joshua, the essential instruction was to meditate on the Word of God "day and night." It meant he had to keep his mind focused on the Word even during his waking moments. If Joshua, a leader of a nation with over a million people, could do this, we can also strive to do the same.

Focus on the Word of God Continuously

We constantly have thoughts occupying our minds. However, it is beneficial to focus our thoughts on God's Word rather than other distractions. I have found it feasible to reflect on the Bible's teachings and contemplate verses while carrying out daily tasks such as work, cleaning the house with my spouse, or fulfilling other responsibilities.

God made our minds to be always active. The things we choose to focus on will dominate our thoughts. In one sense, we can compare our minds to a sponge. If a sponge soaks up water and then is squeezed, water will come out. If you fill your mind with the Word of God, only Scripture will come out when the devil squeezes you.

Many Christians find it challenging to maintain a good relationship with God because of what they choose to focus their minds on. Suppose we spend time consuming worldly knowledge from TV shows, news articles, and sports events. Our minds will become filled with negativity and be vulnerable to the enemy's attacks. To live a fulfilling life with God, we must prioritize filling our minds with His Word, which is full of life and strength.

You Cannot Prioritize Fleshly Desires and Succeed Spiritually

It's widely accepted that it takes more work to concentrate on two things at a time. While some claim to be great at multitasking, they are likely only focused on one task at a time, even if they are switching between two tasks. Essentially, they only focus on the task currently in front of them.

Focusing on Scripture and the events in our daily lives can be equally challenging. It's tough to focus on the Lord while battling doubts and discouragement. Paul tackles this issue in Galatians 5:16–17.

> I say then: Walk in the Spirit, and you shall not fulfill the lust of the flesh. For the flesh lusts against the Spirit, and the Spirit against the flesh; and these are contrary to one another, so that you do not do the things that you wish.

These verses suggest that it's unfeasible to prioritize worldly desires and attain spiritual success. It's not that God won't intervene in our lives; instead, we won't receive His blessings because we haven't aligned ourselves with Him. By prioritizing worldly matters over God, our lives will be misaligned.

Prayer and Meditation

If you're wondering how to practice meditation regularly, the author of Psalm 5 offers some helpful insight.

> Give ear to my words, O Lord,
> Consider my meditation.
> Give heed to the voice of my cry,
> My King and my God,
> For to You I will pray.
> (Psalm 5:1–2)

It's worth noting that he's discussing prayer and meditation, which some people find challenging to comprehend. Essentially, prayer and meditation are interchangeable. Prayer can be regarded as a type of meditation, and meditation can be seen as a type of prayer.

Religious traditions dictate prayer protocols, but some Christians feel restricted by them. Some ministers have taught that specific positions and hand gestures are necessary for God to accept prayer. However, this is not accurate.

Prayer, at its core, is simply a conversation that you or I have with God. Just as I don't need to kneel or fold my hands to talk to my wife, I can communicate with God anytime and anywhere—at home, in the car, or at the store. God wants us to have an ongoing conversation with Him to discuss His Word, our daily lives, and any challenges we may be facing.

Practice Meditation Continuously

No matter where you are, you can connect with God. The Holy Spirit is always present with you—every hour of every day. The Spirit is communicating with us continuously (2 Corinthians 13:14).

Praying doesn't require hiding in a closet away from the world. God doesn't expect us to pray all the time. Instead, we should share His goodness with the world around us. We can't do that if we stay hidden in our closets.

It is possible to develop a constant awareness of the Spirit's presence. He is continually communicating with us. Many will never experience intimacy with Him because they are not listening. Most have not been taught that they can discern His voice, let alone how to discern it.

As Christians, meditation plays an essential role in our spiritual journey. When we pray, we focus our thoughts on God. This practice can be done anytime, anywhere—even while working or doing chores. You may think about personal issues, such as unpaid bills or medical conditions, while at work. In these moments, you are meditating on those things. Shifting our attention to God and integrating this practice into our daily work routine is equally simple.

The Spiritual Battleground

The main idea I want to convey is that when you immerse yourself in God's Word, it can become the primary focus of your thoughts. Some Christians may not believe this is possible, but I assure you that it is, and I am confident that you can achieve this in your own life.

We fight our spiritual battles primarily in our thoughts. Paul explains how this occurs in 2 Corinthians 10:3–6:

> For though we walk in the flesh, we do not war according to the flesh. For the weapons of our warfare *are* not carnal

but mighty in God for pulling down strongholds, casting down arguments and every high thing that exalts itself against the knowledge of God, bringing every thought into captivity to the obedience of Christ, and being ready to punish all disobedience when your obedience is fulfilled.

These verses from Paul contain essential truths that we should understand. They show us that we can have control over our thoughts with God's Word. To achieve this, we must practice meditation regularly and train our minds to focus on godly things throughout the day. Satan's main objective is to infiltrate our thoughts, but we can prevent this by committing ourselves to meditating on Scripture.

Chapter 11

A Foundation in God's Word Will Lead to Spiritual Success

> *For those who live according to the flesh set their minds on the things of the flesh, but those who live according to the Spirit, the things of the Spirit. For to be carnally minded is death, but to be spiritually minded is life and peace. Because the carnal mind is enmity against God; for it is not subject to the law of God, nor indeed can be. So then, those who are in the flesh cannot please God.*
>
> ROMANS 8:5–8

Individuals with carnal minds prioritize their physical senses over God, relying heavily on taste, sight, touch, smell, and hearing instead of following His teachings. As a result, they may only experience small glimpses of God's power in their lives. Christians seeking a deeper connection with God strive to overcome their carnal mind and fully experience His power.

Avoiding Worldly Thinking

Some Christians allow their worldly desires to take over, which prevents them from experiencing the power of God and living a victorious life. Many Christians lack spiritual understanding of their relationship with their creator. On the other hand, those who live according to God's Word receive revelation knowledge and experience His power in their lives. Those who live in a relationship with the Spirit of God will not be controlled by their flesh but rather by God's Word, as the Spirit always aligns with Scripture. Unfortunately, this truth is often overlooked because many teachings in the church focus on the worldly mindset.

According to Paul in Romans 8:6, having a carnal mindset can lead to death. This means that someone focused only on worldly desires cannot receive anything from God. While many Christian teachings concentrate on this, it is important to also acknowledge that it is nearly impossible to receive anything from Satan while maintaining a spiritual perspective. A spiritual and carnal mindset cannot simultaneously dominate a person.

A Christian who prioritizes spirituality is focused on the Word of God throughout the day, from morning to night. If we adopt this mindset, most of our problems will cease, our failures will turn into successes, and the church will start experiencing the power described in Acts.

How to Strengthen Our Faith

The Bible offers guidance on how to strengthen our faith. According to Paul in Romans 10:17, faith comes from hearing the Word of God. We must first become familiar with Scripture through meditation and thoughtful reflection to benefit from it.

According to 2 Peter 1:3, God has already provided us with everything we need for life and godliness. Over the years, I have heard people express their difficulties with faith. Peter emphasizes that the root of this problem is a lack of knowledge. Tapping into God's power and provision is impossible without a revelation of His Word.

Some people who attend our churches may never see God's power manifest because religious beliefs suggest God no longer provides healing or prosperity in present times. As a result, they may struggle to fully believe in God's ability to heal them. This lack of conviction is often due to a lack of knowledge and revelation of God's teachings in the Bible.

The Foundation of Unbelief

Having a solid revelation of Scripture is crucial to standing firm in faith. However, the same applies to doubt and unbelief, which require a solid foundation in the devil's ways and operations. When individuals know how he operates, they are less likely to fall prey to his attacks. Despite what many Christians believe, Satan cannot overpower us easily. He must persuade us to submit to him before his influence over us can take hold.

Our society is inundated with various factors contributing to our belief in the inevitability of sickness, which Satan uses to erode our faith. These factors include commercials on television and seasons designated by society for illnesses like the flu or the common cold. It's hard to imagine Adam and Eve in the garden discussing their vaccination status before the flu season began. Over the centuries, humanity has undergone extensive conditioning that has reinforced our belief in the power of sickness and disease to afflict us.

Before the fall, Adam and Eve lived without knowledge of sickness or poverty. They didn't have a retirement plan or rely on an employer for their needs. Their bodies did not age, so they didn't have to worry about home health care in old age. I see their lives as a representation of God's intention for humanity.

A Functional Knowledge of Sin

Before Adam and Eve's first sin, we did not have a functional knowledge of sin. We currently possess more medical knowledge about diseases like cancer than ever before. However, despite this knowledge, cancer rates continue to rise, which is unexpected. One reason could be that our faith in cancer has increased proportionately to our understanding of the disease, but this has not resulted in a decrease in case counts.

Commercials about cancer are prevalent on TV and can cause fear in many people. It's understandable since we are constantly exposed to them. However, it's worth noting that there are other things we may not fear, such as the "boils" mentioned in Deuteronomy 28, simply because we don't know what they are.

Our Tongue Holds the Power of Life and Death

According to Proverbs 18:21, what we say and hear can release life or death into our lives. This means that the words we use and the information we receive can either help us thrive or harm us. While we often hear about cancer and its harmful effects, we don't hear as much about other illnesses like boils. The number of reported disease cases reflects how much we know and talk about that ailment. As our awareness of the disease increases, so do the number of reported cases.

Few Christians have any level of revelation concerning the power of their tongues. You will find that where knowledge of tragedy and sickness abounds, there are higher levels of doubt and unbelief. As doubt and unbelief increase, the door for Satan to work increases. The inverse is also true. As faith and belief increase, the door for God to work will also increase.

In Romans 16:19, Paul encouraged his readers to know what is "good" and "simple" in their understanding of evil. This wisdom helps protect us from being controlled by Satan. Conversely, when we know God's ways, we can live the life His Spirit directs. As we saw in 2 Peter 1:3, knowing the Lord gives us everything we need to live a fulfilling life.

Chapter 12

God Speaks to Us through His Word

"My sheep hear My voice, and I know them, and they follow Me."
JOHN 10:27

Have you ever wondered how to distinguish the voice of the Lord from the voice of the devil? Many people struggle with this question because they have not been taught to discern God's voice. People often share what the devil has told them because they cannot recognize the source.

Prioritizing the Voice of God

As Christians, it's crucial to prioritize listening to God's voice over the devil's voice. However, many of us struggle with this because of what we choose to focus on. If we spend our waking hours listening to our desires, external factors, or Satan, we won't be able to hear God's voice. Unfortunately, most of our education and teachings come from worldly sources, and only a few Christians seem to be actively seeking to renew themselves with God's wisdom. This lack of focus on God's teachings is likely contributing to the decline of miraculous demonstrations in the church.

According to Jesus, His followers should listen to His voice. Recognizing God's voice is not hard once we learn how to do it. He speaks to us through His Word, thoughts, ideas, or a still, small voice within our spirit that is not audible to our ears. We struggle in this area because we need to spend more time daily meditating on Scripture and being still in His presence. Unfortunately, many Christians are too distracted by the demands of life to do so.

Tuning into God's Voice

With dedication, we can tune ourselves to God's voice to the point where Satan's influence becomes negligible. This will require effort; we may need to turn off the television and possibly sacrifice our favorite sports events to seek God. This is a steep cost to some, but can you imagine the regret of missing a game compared to the eternal rewards in heaven you may receive from missing that game?

Meditation is crucial for Christians to hear God's voice. People struggle with hearing Him because they have been meditating on worldly things. Meditation is essential for learning and understanding any subject in the natural or spiritual realms.

In Mark 4, Jesus discusses the parable of the sower and explains that the seed represents the Word of God. To fully absorb and understand this, we must meditate on Scripture and allow the Holy Spirit to provide insight and deepen our connection to the Word. By doing this, you can firmly plant the seed in your soul and lay the foundation for revelation knowledge.

Are We Giving Ourselves to the Word of God?

Attaining revelation knowledge only sometimes requires reading lengthy passages of Scripture. The Holy Spirit may guide us to concentrate on a specific chapter, book, or even just a few verses. Though they did not have access to various versions of Scripture, commentaries, and teachings like we do today, Paul, Peter, and the apostles operated in greater power due to their revelation of the gospel of Jesus Christ.

> Now in those days, when the number of the disciples was multiplying, there arose a complaint against the Hebrews by the Hellenists, because their widows were neglected in the daily distribution. Then the twelve summoned the multitude of the disciples and said, "It is not desirable that we should leave the word of God and serve tables. Therefore, brethren, seek out from among you seven men of good reputation, full of the Holy Spirit and wisdom, whom we may appoint over this business; but we will give ourselves continually to prayer and to the ministry of the word." And the saying pleased the whole multitude. And they chose Stephen, a man full of faith and the Holy Spirit, and Philip, Prochorus, Nicanor, Timon, Parmenas, and Nicolas, a proselyte from Antioch, whom they set before the apostles; and when they had prayed, they laid hands on them. Then the word of God spread, and the number of the disciples multiplied greatly in Jerusalem, and a great many of the priests were obedient to the faith. (Acts 6:1–7)

The way we think about ministry nowadays is not the same as it was in the early church. In Acts 6:2, the disciples expressed that neglecting God's Word to tend to physical matters was inappropriate. At that time, they did not have access to the Old Testament Scriptures outside the synagogue. So, when they talked about the "word," they were referring to the teachings of Jesus.

It's important to know that meditation essentially means being immersed in the Word of God. We begin by reading the Scriptures and then reflect on what we've read. The aim of this practice is to internalize God's Word in our hearts. I believe the disciples had a similar understanding when they discussed giving themselves "continually to prayer and to the ministry of the word" (Acts 6:4).

Have We Become Deficient in Meditation?

I believe that meditation is an underdeveloped aspect of church practice nowadays. Due to our hectic schedules, we often neglect to reflect and pray over what we learn in church. Instead of taking the time to absorb and understand each verse of the Bible with the guidance of the Holy Spirit, we tend to read it in a rush to cover more content. It is almost as if we expect God to reward us with a prize for ingesting the most significant amounts of Scripture!

Meditation involves deeply contemplating a concept until it becomes fully ingrained in our hearts. While we may be adept at this when it comes to worldly matters, we often struggle with spiritual ones. However, if we devote time to meditating on Scripture, the Holy Spirit can impart revelation knowledge even for the most challenging passages. While we can never fully grasp all the truths in Scripture, meditation can lead us to a deeper understanding than we ever thought possible. For instance, we may gain insights that previously eluded us by going over passages in the Word, such as when we've watched a movie multiple times or scrutinized a bill we couldn't pay.

God chose Joshua to take on Moses's role and lead Israel from the wilderness into the Promised Land. We see in the following verses that mediation would be crucial for his success:

"Only be strong and very courageous, that you may observe to do according to all the law which Moses My servant commanded you; do not turn from it to the right hand or to the left, that you may prosper wherever you go. This Book of the Law shall not depart from your mouth, but you shall meditate in it day and night, that you may observe to do according to all that is written in it. For then you will make your way prosperous, and then you will have good success." (Joshua 1:7–8)

While Joshua only had access to the first five books of Scripture, we are fortunate to have all sixty-six books of the Bible available today. Despite this, the instructions provided in these verses remain just as relevant for us. By regularly meditating on God's Word, day and night, we can become active "doers of the word," as outlined in James 1:22.

Chapter 13

Allowing the Word of God to Dominate Our Lives

"This Book of the Law shall not depart from your mouth, but you shall meditate in it day and night, that you may observe to do according to all that is written in it. For then you will make your way prosperous, and then you will have good success."

JOSHUA 1:8

If we saturate our thoughts with the teachings of the Bible, we will experience the impact of its power. By adopting a lifestyle that reflects the Word of God, we can demonstrate its impact on our lives through our actions and words.

The Benefits of Meditating on the Word

Numerous Christians long for revival and the Holy Spirit's presence in their churches. However, they fail to comprehend that the Holy Spirit already resides within them and awaits their submission to the Word of God to govern their lives.

Over the years, I've heard people discuss their challenges with habits and behaviors that don't glorify God but persist in their lives. Joshua reminds us that without meditating on the Word of God "day and night," it is impossible to "observe to do according to all that is written" (Joshua 1:8). If you dedicate yourself entirely to the Word of God, the things you've struggled with most will gradually disappear.

By devoting ourselves to meditation on the Word of God, we can achieve prosperity and success in life. However, this also means that we are solely responsible for our success, as God has already given us His Word. We must decide whether to settle for the status quo or fully commit to achieving our goals.

Becoming Dominated by the Word of God

By immersing yourself in the Word of God, you can achieve true freedom. However, the decision to do so rests solely with you. It demands a dedication to reflecting on God's promises consistently, day and night. As Joshua explained, those who fail to do this are unlikely to attain "good success" (Joshua 1:8). The psalmist refers to this as setting our delight "in the law of the LORD":

> Blessed is the man
> Who walks not in the counsel of the ungodly,
> Nor stands in the path of sinners,
> Nor sits in the seat of the scornful;
> But his delight is in the law of the LORD,
> And in His law he meditates day and night.
> He shall be like a tree
> Planted by the rivers of water,
> That brings forth its fruit in its season,
> Whose leaf also shall not wither;
> And whatever he does shall prosper.
>   (Psalm 1:1–3)

These verses reiterate the importance of meditating on the Word of God "day and night." Despite this, some Christians overlook the second verse. It's vital to note that the blessings promised in verse 3 cannot be experienced by meditating on news headlines, sports events, or TV shows.

According to the psalmist, it's impossible to simultaneously follow God's blessings and the advice of ungodly people. These are uncertain times with inflation, shortages in critical supplies, and companies downsizing. The ungodly are facing difficulties. However, God will provide for Christians who rely on Him instead of harmful sources like daily news headlines and friends.

Believers should not worry about economic problems like unbelievers because God has promised to provide for His children. He is not limited in His ability to meet our needs, and heaven has no scarcity. By focusing on the Word of God instead of negative news, we can achieve good success even in challenging times. Unfortunately, many Christians spend too much time dwelling on worldly events and end up living like their non-believing neighbors.

When I started serving God, I found it hard to accept that any lack of prosperity in my life was solely my responsibility. I learned that focusing on the wrong things caused this lack in the Christian world. It's important to understand that God has already provided for all our needs (2 Peter 1:3). Still, we need to seek revelation from His Word to change our situation. Ultimately, it's up to us to take action and make the necessary changes.

Have We Disconnected Ourselves from the Word?

It's important to acknowledge that our lives will only change if we regularly engage with the Word. Simply reading it isn't enough. Reading

Scripture while focusing on our problems is possible, but doing so will yield a negative result. The key is actively meditating on the Word rather than passively reading it.

I used to read lists of Scriptures centered around one topic, like healing, once a day. However, I realized I was focusing only on the list rather than the truths within each verse. Instead, I started paying attention to the verses that the Holy Spirit was bringing to my attention. This helped me better absorb and internalize the meaning behind the scriptures. It also created a foundation for revelation knowledge.

Fully Commit to God's Word

To achieve success in the kingdom of God, it is essential to fully commit to allowing His Word to dominate your life. Casually reading Scripture will not suffice, and spending our time reading commentaries and relying on the findings of others to understand Scripture will not either. To prioritize the Word, it must be continuously in your thoughts. You should ponder what God is teaching you day and night. Only when you meditate on the Word at this level will it lead to prosperity.

Most of us have gained an intellectual understanding of Scripture through study, which I call acquired knowledge. However, developing intimacy with God requires a serious commitment of time and energy, similar to a relationship with another person. To better understand, let me provide you with an example.

> Now hope does not disappoint, because the love of God has been poured out in our hearts by the Holy Spirit who was given to us. (Romans 5:5)

Taking time every day to reflect on God's love for you can significantly improve your life. For example, His love enables us to look for the best in other people. How would it affect your work environment if you only saw the good in your coworkers? According to Paul in 2 Corinthians 10:3–5, we can reject negative thoughts and imaginations. However, many of us still need to develop the discipline to do so.

The Power of Our Thoughts

It's essential to control our thoughts through meditation on God's Word. Start by making it a daily practice for at least an hour. Initially, you may struggle to concentrate and only meditate for fifteen minutes. Training your mind to be still and focus on God takes time, but it's necessary to start somewhere.

Christianity today seems to be lacking the power seen in Jesus' and the disciples' ministries. This may be attributed to neglecting to study Scripture and discipline our minds with a dependence on the Spirit of God. We tend to consume the same forms of media as those who don't follow a godly path, such as TV shows, movies, and news. As a result, it's not unexpected that our lives resemble those of our ungodly neighbors.

In Romans 8:5–7, Paul distinguishes between spiritual and carnal mindsets:

> For those who live according to the flesh set their minds on the things of the flesh, but those who live according to the Spirit, the things of the Spirit. For to be carnally minded is death, but to be spiritually minded is life and peace. Because the carnal mind is enmity against God; for it is not subject to the law of God, nor indeed can be.

According to Paul, having a spiritual mindset will bring "life and peace." However, some Christians may find peace difficult if they don't let God's Word guide their lives. You can break free from the endless cycle of tests and trials by changing your focus.

Chapter 14

Harnessing Our Imaginations with God's Word

For though we walk in the flesh, we do not war according to the flesh. For the weapons of our warfare are not carnal but mighty in God for pulling down strongholds, casting down arguments and every high thing that exalts itself against the knowledge of God, bringing every thought into captivity to the obedience of Christ, and being ready to punish all disobedience when your obedience is fulfilled.

2 CORINTHIANS 10:3–6

There is a misunderstanding about the role of imagination today, particularly among Christians. Some believe it can be used for evil, while others haven't considered its potential to tap into the power of God. Although it can advance Satan's goals, it can also be a potent tool when surrendered to the Holy Spirit.

We Lean on Our Imaginations Each Day

We rely on our imagination every day, even when making plans. Since we have yet to experience tomorrow, we must use our imagination to visualize how it might unfold. This helps us create a plan for what we want to accomplish.

People think in pictures and use their imaginations to do so. Imaginations are not evil when used correctly for God's purposes. None of us can fathom what it would be like to live without our imaginations. Can you imagine what it would be like to receive directions without being able to picture the route in your mind?

Imagination plays an important role in meditating on a subject, particularly God's Word. For instance, take John 14:12, where Jesus tells His disciples that not only will they do the works He did, but even greater ones. It's hard for most people to picture themselves doing the works of Jesus because they need to spend more time meditating on the verse.

What Is Meditation?

Meditation involves thoughtful consideration of a subject, such as a Bible verse, chapter, or book. Many people read quickly and only gain intellectual knowledge. Still, those who take the time to slow down and visualize themselves acting out or possessing what they read can gain a deeper understanding. For instance, have you ever paused while reading the Gospels and imagined yourself calling Lazarus out of the grave or feeding the multitudes? This kind of meditation can lead to revelation knowledge.

Jesus said that His followers would do the same works He did. However, many Christians struggle to embrace their new nature and still identify with their old one. Therefore, some may feel uneasy about calling Lazarus from the grave. While it's easy to imagine Jesus performing such a miracle, can you envision yourself doing the same?

In Colossians 1:27, Paul explains that God wants to reveal the richness and glory of a mystery to the world through us. This mystery is "Christ in you." Have you ever considered that Jesus is living in your spirit? While many speak of this, only some have truly internalized this truth. Those who have yet to meditate on this concept may struggle in their Christian journey. It is vital to reach a level of revelation in understanding this simple truth.

Everything Begins with a Vision

According to the writer of Proverbs, having a vision is crucial to avoiding destruction (Proverbs 29:18). To start off, having a vision requires surrendering our imaginations to the Holy Spirit. Vision and imagination go hand in hand, and they can both lead to positive or negative outcomes. Therefore, we should let the Holy Spirit guide our imaginations and impart His vision.

Meditation is a mental exercise that involves thinking. For instance, if I asked you to describe a dog or cat, you would visualize a dog or cat you own. We all think in pictures, but we must focus on controlling what triggers these mental images.

Many Christians do not set aside time to meditate on God's Word daily. As a result, they may have difficulty imagining themselves receiving the promises outlined in Scripture and applying those teachings to their everyday lives. They will also struggle to understand God's vision for their life.

What Are You Meditating On?

It is an unfortunate truth that in the natural realm we all can relate to Satan and his ungodly systems. All of us are familiar with sickness. We have experienced it, and most of us have had someone close die due to it. Commercials on our televisions focus on medications for diseases. Most of us spend more time meditating on these things than on the Word of God.

We can use the local news as an illustration. Finding a broadcast not filled with negative updates is becoming increasingly difficult. The commercials often worsen as they discuss one disease after another with associated medicines. Few people realize that sitting mesmerized in front of the boob tube is a form of meditation.

Conformed to This World?

Paul warned his readers about the danger of becoming conformed to the world around them (Romans 12:2). The word *conformed* paints a picture of something being pressed into a mold. I think of a butter mold when reading the verse. The mold will embed its shape into the butter. The butter will emerge looking just like the pattern in the mold. Similarly, a conformed Christian will emerge from the world's mold looking just like the unbelievers around them.

Some people may see us as strange when we speak the Word over our illnesses. This is because society has become accustomed to sickness and disease and has replaced Scripture with television, movies, and sports. Unfortunately, even Christians have conformed to this societal norm, despite Paul's warning in Romans 12:2.

Accessing God's Provision

According to Peter, God has already made provisions for all aspects of life and godliness (2 Peter 1:3). We can access these provisions by gaining knowledge from God's Word through revelation imparted by the Spirit. However, I have observed that many Christians do not spend enough time meditating on Scripture to develop a vision of themselves living with all their needs met by God.

The positive aspect is that you can meditate on God's Word until it becomes the primary focus of your mind. By renewing your thoughts, it becomes simpler to associate with healing and abundance rather than illness and scarcity. This process will require effort and detachment from gadgets like televisions and mobile phones, but it can be achieved if you decide to do so.

By meditating on the Word of God day and night, we can transform our thoughts and shift our focus to divine health rather than sickness. As a result, we can become so strong in our revelation of healing that we are uncomfortable with physical symptoms that contradict our internal picture. Ultimately, the choice is ours, and our commitment to this practice will determine the outcome.

Chapter 15

Satan Seeks to Steal the Word from Our Hearts

And He said to them, "To you it has been given to know the mystery of the kingdom of God; but to those who are outside, all things come in parables, so that

*'Seeing they may see and not perceive,
And hearing they may hear and not understand;
Lest they should turn,
And their sins be forgiven them.'"*

And He said to them, "Do you not understand this parable? How then will you understand all the parables? The sower sows the word."

MARK 4:11–14

This chapter will focus on understanding the Word of God based on Jesus' teachings in the parable of the sower. Some individuals struggle to comprehend this teaching, but Jesus Himself emphasized its significance in helping us understand His teachings (Mark 4:13). Essentially, the Word of God serves as the ultimate key to unlocking all Scripture. Moreover, Jesus provides us with a roadmap in this parable that can help us access the revelation knowledge we have previously discussed.

The Rosetta Stone

The Rosetta Stone, discovered by Pierre-François Bouchard in 1799, contains three versions of a decree believed to have been issued by King Ptolemy Epiphanes in Egypt. The stone's significance lies in that two versions were written in languages known to scholars. In contrast, the third was written in Egyptian hieroglyphs, which were previously thought to be indecipherable. The ability to decipher the hieroglyphs allowed for a deeper understanding of ancient Egyptian writings.

In Mark 4:13, Jesus informed His disciples that understanding the parable of the sower would enable them to comprehend all of His parables. This parable serves as a Rosetta Stone for Christianity. The principle of seedtime and harvest is present throughout Scripture, starting with Genesis 8:22, which states that it will never cease. We will see that everything in the kingdom of God operates by this principle.

Four Conditions of the Heart

The parable describes four types of soil. The first type represents a person's heart where the Word is planted, but Satan quickly snatches it away before it can take root (Mark 4:16). Matthew's version of the parable provides further insight:

> "When anyone hears the word of the kingdom, and does not understand *it*, then the wicked *one* comes and snatches away what was sown in his heart. This is he who received seed by the wayside." (Matthew 13:19)

Jesus tells us that the condition for Satan stealing the Word is a lack of understanding. I believe He is referencing much more than something resulting from acquired knowledge. If we do not press into the Word we've heard until it becomes a revelation, Satan can steal it from us before we gain any benefit.

The second type of ground represents the heart of a person who excitedly hears the Word of God (Mark 4:16–17). This person may sit in service each week shouting "Amen!" during the preacher's sermon. Unfortunately, they do not expend the necessary effort to ensure the Word they've heard becomes rooted in their heart. Satan will send "tribulation or persecution" into our lives because of the Word we've heard. The ones who have not paid the price to get it rooted deep in their hearts will "stumble" amid the storms of life.

I believe the third type of ground describes the position far too many Christians are in today. It represents the person who listens to the Word but is distracted by the cares of life or their pursuit of other things. Our work, a family situation, or news headlines may pull us away from the Word. Regardless of what it is, Jesus tells us the result is the Word of God will be "unfruitful" in our lives (Mark 4:19).

Finally, the fourth type of ground represents those who "hear" the Word of God and produce fruit. These are the people who will press into the things of God until they become revelation knowledge.

Jesus shares a parable explaining why the Word of God might not produce results in our lives. By examining the four types of ground, we can understand why we may not be seeing the fruit we desire. It's essential to meditate on the Word's truths and keep them at the forefront of our minds to fulfill God's plan for our lives.

Corruptible and Incorruptible Seeds

According to Peter, we are reborn through the "incorruptible" seed of God's Word (1 Peter 1:23). Similarly, Paul notes that this seed is implanted in our hearts when we hear God's Word (Romans 10:17), meaning that our tongues are the mechanism for planting the seed of Scripture into our hearts.

The writer of Proverbs tells us that "death and life" are in the power of our tongues (Proverbs 18:21). Peter also references the concepts of "corruptible" and "incorruptible" seeds in his first letter (1 Peter 1:23), indicating that every word we allow into our ears can produce a harvest of either life or death.

Through personal experience, I have discovered that the two main ways we plant "seeds" into our hearts are through what we hear and see. Essentially, everything we listen to or watch has the potential to plant seeds that are either corruptible or incorruptible in our hearts—this includes television shows, movies, news broadcasts, and songs.

How to Plant the Word in Your Heart

Many people have asked me how to plant the Word of God in their hearts. Jesus teaches us that the "sower sows the word" (Mark 4:14). Therefore, my answer is always the same: you need to plant the Word by either reading it or listening to it.

This parable contains so many truths it could fill a book. We will only be able to explore some of them. Meditating on the parable allows the Spirit to reveal additional truths.

Unfortunately, many Christians do not understand these things. They believe their battles will end once they receive salvation and become a new creation in Christ Jesus. Some even think that they will never face discouragement, sickness, or lack again in their lives. However, this is not true. Satan targets those who start discovering the revelation of Jesus Christ (Galatians 1:12) and does everything in his power to prevent the Word of God from taking root in our hearts.

Guarding Our Hearts

I once heard someone ask a minister why they should bother trying to understand Scripture if Satan could steal it from them (Matthew 13:19). The person believed that if they never gained any revelation of the Word and just accepted a defeated life, Satan would ignore them. However, they needed correction. If someone gains revelation knowledge and truly understands the spiritual truths in Scripture, Satan cannot steal the Word from them.

The parable of the sower applies to all Christians, including ministers. Ministers are not exempt from life's problems, and Satan works harder to steal the Word from them due to their influence over others. It's essential to remain vigilant, as Satan will never stop trying to destroy us. He understands the principles we've discussed and uses seemingly harmless things like our favorite sitcoms, movies, or songs to plant corruptible seeds in our hearts. Each one will produce a result.

Consider the following guidance provided in the book of Proverbs:

> My son, give attention to my words;
> Incline your ear to my sayings.
> Do not let them depart from your eyes;
> Keep them in the midst of your heart;
> For they *are* life to those who find them,
> And health to all their flesh.
> Keep your heart with all diligence,
> For out of it *spring* the issues of life.
> Put away from you a deceitful mouth,
> And put perverse lips far from you.
> Let your eyes look straight ahead,
> And your eyelids look right before you.
> Ponder the path of your feet,
> And let all your ways be established.
> (Proverbs 4:20–26)

The parable of the sower offers practical advice for our spiritual journey. To keep our hearts pure, we must focus on God's Word and be mindful of what we see and hear. This requires us to pay attention and carefully choose what we listen to and look at every moment of every day.

Chapter 16

Following the Spirit as We Sow the Seeds of God's Word

"The sower sows the word. And these are the ones by the wayside where the word is sown. When they hear, Satan comes immediately and takes away the word that was sown in their hearts. These likewise are the ones sown on stony ground who, when they hear the word, immediately receive it with gladness; and they have no root in themselves, and so endure only for a time. Afterward, when tribulation or persecution arises for the word's sake, immediately they stumble. Now these are the ones sown among thorns; they are the ones who hear the word, and the cares of this world, the deceitfulness of riches, and the desires for other things entering in choke the word, and it becomes unfruitful. But these are the ones sown on good ground, those who hear the word, accept it, and bear fruit: some thirtyfold, some sixty, and some a hundred."

MARK 4:14–20

Some individuals think that genuinely spiritual people will never encounter trials or difficulties. However, I wonder whether they have familiarized themselves with Jesus' explanation of the parable of the sower. This story demonstrates that Satan will oppose our efforts to establish a strong connection with God's Word. He recognizes the threat a person with a renewed mindset presents to his objectives.

Looking beyond Our Five Physical Senses

Relying solely on our physical senses for guidance can be misleading. To avoid this, Paul advised his readers in Rome to allow the Holy Spirit to lead them (Romans 8:14). As Christians, the Holy Spirit resides within us and desires to guide us in all aspects of life. We can significantly benefit by training ourselves to seek His guidance in every situation.

Unfortunately, many Christians do not recognize the Holy Spirit as a helper. Instead, they view Him as a supernatural phenomenon that manifests only during church services. I believe it's essential for every Christian to meditate on Jesus' teachings about the Spirit, which are recorded in chapters 14 to 16 of John.

Choking the Life from Satan's Corruptible Seeds

We spoke in the previous chapter about incorruptible and corruptible seeds. Satan will look for every opportunity to steal the Word from us. Corruptible seeds are one of his primary ways of doing so. These will produce spiritual thorns capable of choking the life out of any incorruptible seeds that have been planted.

Jesus told His disciples that "the cares of this world, the deceitfulness of riches, and the desires for other things" would "choke the word" (Mark 4:19) that has been sown in their hearts. Do you think the same thing can happen to the fruit of Satan's corruptible seeds if we focus on ensuring only incorruptible seeds are planted? This will result in the life of those corruptible seeds being cut off, causing them to wither and die.

Moving beyond Other People's Opinions

One particularly successful tactic Satan uses to plant corruptible seeds in our lives is other people's opinions. Many of us have fallen into this trap. Can you imagine what Jesus' ministry would have been like if He had worried about what people thought of Him?

Jesus did not expend effort researching target markets or evaluating how people responded to His messages. His focus instead was on doing the Father's will. He even said that He only spoke the things taught to Him by the Father (John 8:28). How different do you think our ministries would be if we followed His example?

Jesus' own family turned against Him, and He still pressed forward into the Father's plan for His life and ministry. Do you think we would be willing to choose the plan of God over even our families if pressed to do so?

Jesus always put His Father's will above His own. He was totally surrendered, and as a result, miraculous manifestations occurred wherever He ministered. Jesus never missed the will of God once.

Are We Chasing Crowds or God's Will?

The Lord asked me a simple question when we began production of our weekly television program. He asked whether it would be enough if no one except Him watched the broadcasts. I was taken aback at first by this question. Wasn't the goal to build a platform capable of reaching the masses for His kingdom? He showed me that it was not. Instead, His purpose was for us to produce the program with teaching that He directed us to release. Obedience is our role and increase is God's (1 Corinthians 3:6–8).

A herd mentality has overtaken much of our church culture. I believe this is because we do not understand the principle of sowing the Word of God as a seed. Our sole job in the ministry is to plant the seed of God's Word in the hearts of men and women. There are many ways to do this. Some will receive the seed, and some will not. We cannot allow ourselves to become focused on people's opinions over God's.

Many ministers talk about the crowds they are drawing as proof God is moving in their church or ministry. Using crowd size as a gauge, we would almost have to credit the Spirit of God for drawing thousands to mosques and ungodly temples! We would also have to say Jesus' ministry failed because His followers left Him when things turned for the worst and the soldiers came to arrest Him (Mark 14:50).

Paul Chose to Sow the Word Instead of Chase Crowds

There is an interesting account from Paul's ministry recorded in Acts 19:8–10:

> And he went into the synagogue and spoke boldly for three months, reasoning and persuading concerning the things of the kingdom of God. But when some were hardened and did not believe, but spoke evil of the Way before the multitude, he departed from them and withdrew the disciples, reasoning daily in the school of Tyrannus. And this continued for two years, so that all who dwelt in Asia heard the word of the Lord Jesus, both Jews and Greeks.

Paul went into the synagogue and began to preach the gospel when he arrived in Ephesus. Many people who heard him were "hardened and did not believe" (Acts 19:9). How would we have responded to this situation? Our culture is fixated on acceptance. We must never forget Jesus told us that "tribulation and persecution" would follow the sowing of God's Word (Mark 4:17).

There is no indication from the account in Acts 19 that Paul took the people's response personally. He did not argue or try to convince the people, as many of us probably would have. Instead, Paul chose to pull his disciples out of the synagogue. He then spent two years teaching them "in the school of Tyrannus" (Acts 19:9).

I have heard ministers talk about the handkerchiefs taken from Paul's hands that were placed on the sick, which resulted in miraculous healings and deliverances (Acts 19:12). While it is exciting to think about seeing signs and wonders, few of these ministers have ever mentioned the two years Paul spent sowing the Word before he saw the harvest of miraculous signs. We can confidently say that Paul's ministry differed from the church growth movement of our day.

We evaluate the success of our ministries based on measurable outcomes, such as the size of our audience or the prosperity of our preachers. However, I believe that the early church was less concerned with external factors and more focused on following the guidance of the Holy Spirit and spreading the message of God's Word. This passage is just one example that shows nothing else mattered to them. We could look at many other passages to further cement this point.

Paul Relied on the Holy Spirit

Now when they had gone through Phrygia and the region of Galatia, they were forbidden by the Holy Spirit to preach the word in Asia. After they had come to Mysia, they tried to go into Bithynia, but the Spirit did not permit them. So passing by Mysia, they came down to Troas. And a vision appeared to Paul in the night. A man of Macedonia stood and pleaded with him, saying, "Come over to Macedonia and help us." (Acts 16:6–9)

Some individuals may hesitate to act for God without clear direction from Him. However, Paul's example in these verses shows that he did not always rely on specific guidance. Rather than allowing external circumstances to dictate his actions, Paul continued to move forward until the Holy Spirit intervened and redirected his path.

We sit and wait for direction or a particular word of wisdom from God to determine our path. I believed it was wrong to do anything without clear direction until the Holy Spirit opened my eyes to how Paul was led. Many Christians are where I was: stuck and not moving. Paul did not wait for a clear direction but continued until the Spirit redirected him.

Paul was traveling toward Asia when the Holy Spirit stopped him and forbade him to continue. The account makes it clear that Paul did not call his companions to a time of prayer and fasting to receive direction. Paul deflected and started traveling on a new path toward Bithynia until he was again stopped by the Spirit.

After reading Acts 16, I discovered that waiting for a "leading" to share the gospel with someone is not necessary. Jesus has already directed us to go and preach the gospel (Mark 16:15). I now understand that I don't have to wait for God's permission to minister. He has commanded me to go, and I should only refrain if He tells me not to for a particular reason.

Chapter 17

The Word Becomes Power If We Do Not Allow Satan to Steal It

Yes, and all who desire to live godly in Christ Jesus will suffer persecution.

2 TIMOTHY 3:12

I've noticed that some ministers preach that the Lord will eliminate any obstacles the enemy puts in our way. However, they may need to examine what Paul wrote in 2 Timothy. Paul warned Timothy that he would face persecution while following God's plan. He told the Corinthian believers something similar regarding the ministry door opened to him:

> For a great and effective door has opened to me, and *there are* many adversaries. (1 Corinthians 16:9)

Please understand that I am not stating Christians must live in defeat, sickness, or poverty. Instead, my point is that Satan will come against anyone who allows their life to be dominated by the Word of God. He understands that the Word is God's seed and will do everything in his power to keep it from taking root in our hearts. If you decide to pursue God with all your heart, you must accept that persecution will follow.

The Path to Revelation Will Be Filled with Persecution

Paul prayed that God would give the Ephesian Christians "the spirit of wisdom and revelation in the knowledge of Him" (Ephesians 1:17). The "Him" refers to Jesus. I believe the author of Hebrews referred to the revelation of the Lord when speaking of those who are "illuminated" (Hebrews 10:32). Satan is fully aware of the damage a person with this revelation can do to his plans!

Any person who begins to have the eyes of their spiritual understanding opened will have to fight to keep them open. For example, my wife and I were blessed with good health for over ten years. We were immediately attacked with physical issues the moment our hearts became set on pursuing the plan of God. The Holy Spirit has faithfully led us through multiple battles. We will have victory. Our hearts are set, and neither of us will allow Satan to distract us or cause us to draw back from the plan of God.

You cannot avoid the fact that the enemy will attack anyone who starts to walk in truth. The attacks on my health and my wife's health are just one example. His attacks may come from a family illness, financial loss, a car accident, or other tragedies. God is faithful and has sent His Holy Spirit to guide us through every battle. He will not forsake us; we will experience victory if our heart is set and we do not draw back.

My question is whether you will commit with me to press into the Word of God regardless of what storms may come. I believe the only correct path is for us to stand firm in the Word, resisting every attack of Satan. If you do this, I guarantee you'll come through with a shout of victory. It may not happen overnight or next week, but success will come if you commit to standing firm.

God Will Not Test You

I've heard some people suggest that God uses afflictions to test one's commitment to His Word, but this belief is incorrect. James warned his readers against making these claims and emphasized the importance of understanding the Word:.

> Let no one say when he is tempted, "I am tempted by God"; for God cannot be tempted by evil, nor does He Himself tempt anyone. (James 1:13)

It is not in God's nature to intentionally push, test, or humble us through trials. His plans for our lives are always good, but our own actions may hinder Him from providing His blessings. This can happen in various ways, such as through our unbelief, religious traditions, or failure to discipline our desires.

The Word and the Power

Paul tells us the gospel is the power of God (Romans 1:16). He was referring to the entire Bible. We can combine this with Peter's description of the Word as an "incorruptible" seed (1 Peter 1:23). Those two verses combined tell us that the Word of God is an incorruptible power seed. In the context of the parable of the sower, we deduce that any lack of power directly results from the wrong "seed" being consistently planted in our souls.

The challenge you must not forget is that Satan understands these principles. He knows the key to releasing the power of God is consistently planting the Word into our souls. For this reason, he sends things like sickness, work issues, or tragedies to deflect our attention.

There is no difference between you, me, or the apostle Paul. God's Word is a seed that will operate the same for every human being when planted consistently in the heart. The only difference between someone like Peter or Paul and me or you is what they did with the revelation imparted to them by the Holy Spirit.

God has committed His Word to us. It is His precious seed that we consistently plant and then care for to allow time for it to grow and release the life and power of God. We "plant" it while meditating, which we've previously seen is when we set aside everything else to focus on it.

Shut the Door to Satan's Corruptible Seeds

We see in Matthew 13:19 that the person who lacks understanding is a prime target for Satan to steal the Word planted in their heart. Christians are far too sensitive of being criticized or attacked for their beliefs. Satan will use anyone who will yield to him to attack us. Do not forget that his target is the Word that you have received. He is only concerned with keeping it from becoming deeply rooted in your soul.

Paul tells us in 2 Corinthians 10:3–6 that our minds are the battlefield where spiritual warfare is fought. Satan will tirelessly work to plant "corruptible" seeds into our thought lives (1 Peter 1:23). These will produce harvests we do not want to partake in. You and I are the only ones who can resist his efforts by choosing to shut off the conduits of those corruptible seeds.

Change Comes by Sowing the Word Seed

The author of Psalm 119 tells us God's Word "is settled in heaven" (Psalm 119:89). It is the unchanging anchor of our lives in an ever-changing world. Peter called it an "incorruptible seed" (1 Peter 1:23). It will change your life if you consistently plant it in your heart and allow it to become deeply rooted.

In the context of the Word being a seed, let's take a moment to consider a kernel of corn. It can produce a corn harvest if we plant, nurture, and allow the kernel time to grow and develop. The Word of God operates no differently than a kernel of corn.

It will help to look at your Bible like a container of incorruptible seeds. Some of these are healing seeds, some deliverance seeds, and others prosperity seeds. You will find a "seed" in the Bible for every situation or need. Each contains the power of God but, like a natural seed, will provide no benefit until planted in the ground of our hearts.

The Word of God will not produce anything in your life without first being planted. I once had a pastor tell me to place a Bible under my pillow at night to allow time for it to soak into my brain. He was wrong! You can put it under your pillow, on your head, or even stand on it, and nothing will change in your life. It will not produce healing, joy, or victory if we do not plant it in our hearts and give it time to germinate and grow. The primary way this happens is by speaking it and looking at it. Our eyes and ears are the gateways to our hearts through which the seed must pass.

We Need Power, Not Gimmicks

Jesus left us with the commandment to "go" and preach the gospel message (Matthew 28:19–20). He commissioned us to spread His Word seed in the ground of unbelieving hearts. He sent His Spirit to anoint us as we go. Unfortunately, many have gone in their own strength and power. They desire to serve and glorify God but lack the Spirit's anointing and minister only from acquired knowledge.

I have met many men and women over the years who have answered the call of God. They work tirelessly in the ministry with little fruit to show from their labors. The majority talk about God but have no relationship with Him, no accompanying power, and minimal fruit for the kingdom. In most cases, I've noticed these people meet little resistance from Satan because they've unwittingly become tools in his hand to lead people into religious bondage.

It is possible to draw a crowd, get people to repeat a prayer, and still produce little to no spiritual fruit. I know of ministers who will call out specific physical ailments such as cancer, diabetes, or hernias and then declare the healing power of God upon each one. While the Holy Spirit will sometimes provide words of knowledge to a minister regarding specific conditions, in most cases, these ministers are not hearing from Him. They know statistics are on their side and that someone in the crowd will respond. Remember that the Holy Spirit will never require gimmicks to draw people to Jesus!

Chapter 18

The Word Must Take Root in Your Heart to Release Power

And the apostles said to the Lord, "Increase our faith."

So the Lord said, "If you have faith as a mustard seed, you can say to this mulberry tree, 'Be pulled up by the roots and be planted in the sea,' and it would obey you."

LUKE 17:5–6

I often referred to the mustard seed as an example of how even a tiny amount of faith can accomplish great things. Many ministers I heard reinforced this belief. However, my perspective shifted during a Bible study when the leader read from Luke 17:5–6, highlighting that the mustard seed is the smallest of all seeds. At that moment, the Holy Spirit prompted me to consider whether Jesus was referencing the seed's size or something else.

I was surprised when the Spirit prompted me to consider what else Jesus could have been referring to besides the size of the seed. It was clear that I was missing something, so I decided to research mustard seeds in more depth over the next few days. The most interesting thing I learned was that mustard seeds develop taproots that can grow as deep as three to five feet, even in dry conditions, before the first blade emerges.

Through my research, I have come to view Jesus' response to the disciples' request in a new light. While we typically focus on the size of the mustard seed, could Jesus have been alluding to the importance of being deeply grounded in His Word? In this chapter, we will explore the immense power that is available to those who take the time to establish a firm foundation.

Abiding in the Word Is the Key to Revelation Knowledge

Jesus told His followers that they would have to abide in His Word to become His disciples. This means remaining focused on it consistently. It doesn't mean they cannot do anything else, but they must always keep the Word of God in their thoughts—even at work or school.

I once received guidance from the Holy Spirit that a close relationship with Him is linked to having a close relationship with the Word of God. To build this relationship, we must follow Jesus' advice to "abide" in Scripture, which will help us develop a strong foundation of revelation, knowledge, and understanding.

We tend to make much of our natural understanding and ability to learn. The relationship I am talking about will take you beyond acquired knowledge. It is the doorway by which we enter into revelation knowledge that can only be taught by the Holy Spirit.

Knowledge of God's Word Gained through Personal Experience

It's important to remember that the printed Bible is a faithful representation of God's Word. Still, it doesn't become "His Word" until we take the time to internalize it and allow the Holy Spirit to reveal its true meaning. We must immerse ourselves in the Word and make it part of our daily lives.

Jesus promised His followers that they would come to know the truth, but this goes beyond a surface-level understanding of Scripture (John 8:32). It involves developing a deep, personal connection with the truth, leading to a greater revelation and understanding of God's Word. This understanding can help us overcome the challenges we face in life and experience true victory.

Perhaps the idea of being "intimate" with God's Word is unfamiliar. This means developing a relationship through daily time spent reading and studying it. Unfortunately, a lack of intimacy with the Word has led many Christians to live in bondage to illness, disease, and spiritual oppression.

The Seven Sons of Sceva

Attempting to exercise our authority while lacking intimacy with the Holy Spirit and the Word will lead to trouble. We see this in the account of the seven sons of Sceva:

> Then some of the itinerant Jewish exorcists took it upon themselves to call the name of the Lord Jesus over those who had evil spirits, saying, "We exorcise you by the Jesus whom Paul preaches." Also there were seven sons of Sceva, a Jewish chief priest, who did so. And the evil spirit answered and said, "Jesus I know, and Paul I know; but who are you?" Then the man in whom the evil spirit was leaped on them, overpowered them, and prevailed against them, so that they fled out of that house naked and wounded. (Acts 19:13–16)

The seven sons of Sceva had acquired knowledge of Paul's methods for dealing with demons. They did not have any revelation of the authority in which Paul walked. You must never forget that Satan is not intimidated by the written Bible or our acquired knowledge. We can spend hours studying Scripture, memorize whole passages, and then quote those to Satan. His reaction will be no different than it was to Sceva's sons.

The Bible only becomes powerful when we internalize it and allow it to grow within us, providing us with insight and understanding. It is a book of spiritual substance, described by Jesus as "spirit" and "life" (John 6:63), and also likened to a seed (Mark 4:14). However, its power remains dormant until we take it off the page and plant it within our hearts. The Word of God requires the fertile soil of our hearts to germinate, grow, and produce a bountiful harvest of divine power.

Satan Will Fight Our Efforts to Plant God's Word in Our Souls

Earlier, we discussed how four types of ground can represent the state of our hearts. Satan will try to distract us with various forms of temptation, like in the first three types of soil, to divert our focus from the Word of God. Jesus spoke about individuals who get excited about the Word of God but fail to spend enough time abiding in it to allow it to take root in their souls (Mark 4:17). Such individuals are associated with the "stony" type of ground, and their excitement quickly fades away when faced with difficult situations. While it's great to see people enthusiastically shouting "Amen" during sermons, my personal experience has shown me that many of these individuals "have no root" (Mark 4:17), which means they produce minimal or no fruit from what they've heard.

Seeing people give up during difficult times and share negative experiences about how their faith didn't work for them is disheartening. We've all been there, feeling discouraged in our pursuit of God.

However, it's important to remember that just like a natural seed takes time to grow, the "seed" of God's Word takes time to germinate in our souls. If we push through the discouragement and nurture the seeds planted in our hearts through prayer and meditation, victory is guaranteed.

Satan's Target Is the Word Seed Planted in Your Heart

I have heard some ministers discuss reaching a level of intimacy with God where we are impervious to the devil's schemes. However, it's essential to understand that we can never eliminate Satan's influence from our lives. He targets the "seed" of God's Word that we sow in our hearts, and he will always try to steal it before it can take root. While we can strengthen our resistance to him, we will never reach a point where he ceases to threaten our spiritual growth.

I've heard people wonder out loud why they feel like the devil is always targeting them. If you feel the same way, it's likely because he sees you as a vessel for God's Word. He's after the Word, and you just happen to be in the way. Knowing this can help you not take things so personally.

We Are Nothing without Jesus

A minister once said that God has never had anyone work for Him who was qualified for the task. As sinners, we were all destined for hell before we met Jesus. Paul speaks to this in the book of Romans, stating that there is no good in our flesh (Romans 7:18). We should never forget that God chooses people based solely on the blood of Jesus, not their spiritual accomplishments.

In the past, I would read about the "great" individuals of faith in church history and aspire to be like them. Perhaps you have experienced the same desire. However, the Holy Spirit has revealed to me that they were human beings, just like you and me. The only thing that set them apart was their dedication to the Word of God and their relationship with Him. By emulating their actions in these aspects, we can reach the same heights of faith.

It's a common misconception that God plays favorites. In reality, He doesn't choose anyone to be more important than others. Some people experience more of His power because they have studied and meditated on His Word, allowing its truths to take root in their hearts. God anoints His Word, and those who consistently and diligently focus on it will see His blessings in their lives. Ultimately, it's up to us whether or not we allow ourselves to be used by God.

Chapter 19

God's Word Alone Is the Seed That Produces Miracles

And He said, "The kingdom of God is as if a man should scatter seed on the ground, and should sleep by night and rise by day, and the seed should sprout and grow, he himself does not know how. For the earth yields crops by itself: first the blade, then the head, after that the full grain in the head. But when the grain ripens, immediately he puts in the sickle, because the harvest has come."

MARK 4:26–29

It's important to note that God doesn't choose people based on their skills or qualifications. He has no "favorites" who receive special gifts or anointings. Instead, He wants us all to become "good ground" where His Word can take root, grow, and produce a bountiful harvest.

To achieve growth in God's kingdom, it's crucial that we set aside time every day to tend to His Word by planting it in our hearts and nurturing it with prayer. The apostle Paul referred to this as being "transformed by the renewing of your mind" in Romans 12:2.

While many Christians focus on external efforts to change the world, it's important to remember that God's Word, not our efforts, truly brings about change. By planting His Word in our hearts and allowing it to take root, we can experience transformation without even trying. Imagine the impact our ministries could have if we ministered only from minds renewed by the Word of God and focused only on spreading God's Word seed.

Continuous Sowing Produces Continuous Results

According to James, our souls are saved by "the implanted word" (James 1:21). The word translated as "implanted" in Greek is used only in this verse and refers to a seed that has sprouted and grown. Jesus also spoke about the earth producing crops on its own in Mark 4:28, using the metaphor of our souls as the earth. By consistently planting God's Word in our souls daily, we allow it to take root and grow. This practice can lead to the gradual elimination of negative habits and sins as the Word seeds take over and replace the corruptible seeds that were previously planted.

Any seed implanted in our souls will yield results. Jesus referred to this concept in Mark 4:28, and it applies to both incorruptible and corruptible seeds. If you have previously planted corruptible seeds, they can be replaced with God's incorruptible Word seeds. As time passes, these seeds will take root and enable you to flourish like a flower in a desert. Your spirit will overflow with rivers of living water, and communicating with God in prayer will become effortless.

We Cannot Earn God's Favor

God's unconditional love for you cannot be earned through any external actions. His plan for your life was established before you were born, and He sent Jesus to die for your sins before you came into being. You cannot enhance or diminish His love for you in any way.

The Word of God is an incorruptible seed that has the potential to unleash the miraculous power of the Holy Spirit. While it is crucial to make reading and meditating on God's Word a daily practice, it can quickly become a religious routine. Developing a personal relationship with God is more important than religious activities. Plant and nourish the Word of God in your heart to build a deeper connection with Him.

Many people desire to be used by God but approach Him with religious obligations rather than a genuine desire for a relationship. God wants a relationship with us; the anointing we seek will be imparted as we fellowship with Him. Any effort made in His service without a relationship will lead to empty religious traditions. God is not looking for preaching experts or individuals who have polished exteriors. Instead, He desires people willing to invest the time to soak in His Word until they receive revelation knowledge.

Cultivating the Soil of Our Souls

In one of my Bible college classes, the professor highlighted how God chooses to use particular personality types. However, I believe this contradicts Paul's message in 1 Corinthians 1:27, which tells us God uses "foolish things of the world to put to shame the wise." We should remember that God's standards differ from ours, and He qualifies people for service that we may not consider.

To experience the miraculous, we must cultivate the soil of our souls with God's Word. By sowing it into our souls and watering it in prayer, we become a container filled with His Word seed. The Holy Spirit is sent to help us, but the decision to plant and water the seed is ours alone to make. By meditating daily and allowing time for the Word to take root in our souls, we will see a harvest in time.

Unfortunately, for various reasons, not all Christians will sow the Word. There is an endless list of excuses to choose from, such as busyness or lack of understanding. It's time to stop letting distractions hinder us and focus on the Word of God. We do not see more of God's power manifested in the church today because we are not prioritizing His Word.

Satan Will Attempt to Steal the Word before It Takes Root

Jesus warned His disciples that Satan would quickly try to steal the Word that is planted in their hearts (Mark 4:15). It's important to take time to sow the Word, but it's also crucial to prepare against Satan's attempts to take it away. You must be committed to standing your ground and fighting while the Word takes root in your soul. Sadly, many people give up on this fight when the going gets tough, and some even give up on the Word of God altogether.

It has become increasingly clear to me that we will face opposition as we pursue God's will. To bear fruit in the kingdom, we must be firmly committed to standing strong through Satan's storms. It takes a solid backbone to persevere, but the Holy Spirit will be with us every step of the way and give us strength.

People sitting in a bar will not face the same kind of opposition that we do. They may face troubles in their lives, but Satan is not concerned about them because they do not have the Word of God in their hearts. However, those committed to getting the Word rooted in their hearts will face serious opposition from the devil; he will use every means to keep us from pursuing the Word.

Our Relationship with God Is Our Safeguard against Satan

Religious tradition is a tool that Satan uses to steal the Word, and Jesus warned about its dangers (Mark 7:13). To ensure that the Word of God takes deep root in our souls, we must allow ample time for it to grow. Religious traditions can hinder this process and choke the life out of the seed.

So, how can we safeguard ourselves from falling into Satan's traps? The answer is more straightforward than we think: it lies in our relationship with God. Our Christian walk is built on the foundation of our relationship with God. We may stumble and make mistakes while pursuing the Word of God, but we can always find solace in God's unwavering love and support. He will strengthen us each step of the way and send His Spirit to guide us through any distractions Satan throws at us. Rest assured that God will never give up on us and will always be waiting to draw us closer to Him.

Chapter 20

Who Is Trying to Shake Your Commitment to God's Word?

> *"Therefore hear the parable of the sower: When anyone hears the word of the kingdom, and does not understand it, then the wicked one comes and snatches away what was sown in his heart. This is he who received seed by the wayside. But he who received the seed on stony places, this is he who hears the word and immediately receives it with joy; yet he has no root in himself, but endures only for a while. For when tribulation or persecution arises because of the word, immediately he stumbles. Now he who received seed among the thorns is he who hears the word, and the cares of this world and the deceitfulness of riches choke the word, and he becomes unfruitful."*
>
> MATTHEW 13:18–22

Our relationship with God is at the core of the Christian life. Jesus taught that eternal life is achieved through knowing God. However, we must commit ourselves to meditating on and following the Word of God to strengthen this relationship. The Holy Spirit once revealed to me that my level of intimacy with God would not surpass my level of familiarity with His Word. By meditating on Scripture, we deepen our understanding of God and recognize His voice more clearly.

Satan Is Determined to Steal the Word

Achieving victory in the Christian life involves two elements: our relationship with God and our commitment to His Word. These two components are interdependent, and Satan knows this. He will try every possible tactic to undermine our confidence in both.

Satan understands the principle of sowing and reaping. He does not want the Word of God to take root in our hearts. His attacks are often launched through people close to us—such as church members, church staff, friends, or family—who he uses to plant negative thoughts in our minds. Sometimes, we may even have to sever close relationships to protect our hearts.

There are many churches where the Word of God is preached faithfully, but unfortunately this is not the case for all churches. I have met people who attend church regularly but have never heard anything beyond traditional teachings from the pulpit. Satan uses these churches to sow corruptible seeds in the members' hearts. Exposure to such harmful teachings will have a detrimental effect on our spiritual growth. The corruptible seeds associated with them will take root and choke the life from God's Word.

Evil Communications

In 1 Corinthians 15:33, Paul warns his readers about the dangers of associating with evil company. The Greek words in the verse describe how these associations can lead to daily lifestyle patterns that cause us to deviate from a higher level of spirituality. We must beware of teachings that promote unbelief and religious traditions, as they can contain corruptible seeds that lead us toward a carnal lifestyle dominated by our physical senses.

Religious tradition contains corruptible seeds that have caused many to lose faith throughout church history. I have heard people say God called them to churches dominated by tradition. It is beyond me how anyone could believe He would do this. These places will expose their hearts to a continuous stream of corruptible seeds; it is crucial to avoid these churches if our desire is to walk in the miraculous power of God.

Church Tradition and Corruptible Seeds

I want to clarify that I have nothing against local churches. In fact, many deliver the incorruptible seed through their weekly sermons and are filled with passionate people who have knowledge and revelation of the Word. We should strive to be among this group.

Unfortunately, there are some congregations that do not fit the biblical definition of a local church. These groups lead their faithful members into religious traditions and sow corruptible seeds through their messages, which can rob the people of God's miraculous power. In my experience, these groups are often led by well-meaning ministers who lack spiritual understanding and rely solely on acquired knowledge. It's important to recognize when a church has drifted far from the Word. If it has, we must avoid it.

Preach the Revelation of Jesus Christ

In his letter to the Galatian Christians, Paul cautioned his readers about the risks associated with preaching based solely on acquired knowledge:

> But even if we, or an angel from heaven, preach any other gospel to you than what we have preached to you, let him be accursed. As we have said before, so now I say again, if anyone preaches any other gospel to you than what you

have received, let him be accursed. For do I now persuade men, or God? Or do I seek to please men? For if I still pleased men, I would not be a bondservant of Christ. But I make known to you, brethren, that the gospel which was preached by me is not according to man. For I neither received it from man, nor was I taught *it,* but *it came* through the revelation of Jesus Christ. (Galatians 1:8–12)

In verse 8, the author's message is serious. The gospel message can only be understood through the revelation of Jesus Christ, as stated in Galatians 1:12. One cannot gain access to it through academic studies or human effort. I am grateful that God is merciful, and His Spirit will guide us toward revelation knowledge if we acknowledge His presence and look to Him. Without this guidance, many preachers will hesitate to preach the gospel Paul preached, fearing they will not do it correctly.

Guard Your Heart against Corruptible Seeds

Over the years, as I have spent time with the Holy Spirit, these truths have become much clearer to me. Unfortunately, in my earlier years, I was misinformed and listened to ministers who fed me corruptible seeds. The Holy Spirit has guided me throughout my journey, and He will do the same for you.

Paul's letters to churches reveal the revelation of Jesus. I do not suggest we disregard the Old Testament, but we should primarily focus on the New Testament letters. They inform us of who we are in Christ Jesus and our redemptive rights. I suggest you find verses about our position in Christ and write them out in the first person. I provided you example verses in chapter 9 to help you get started.

No church or minister is perfect. Every message we listen to has the potential to have at least some corruptible seeds in the content. Gaining revelation of your position in Christ will protect against these. It will provide you with discernment and enable you to identify any seed you do not want to be planted in your soul. The Holy Spirit has taught me to curse these and apply the blood of Christ to them so they cause no harm and open no door to Satan in my life.

Beware of the Thorns

The third type of ground Jesus described contained thorns capable of choking the life from any incorruptible seeds planted in our hearts:

> "Now these are the ones sown among thorns; they are the ones who hear the word, and the cares of this world, the deceitfulness of riches, and the desires for other things entering in choke the word, and it becomes unfruitful." (Mark 4:18–19)

The word translated as "cares" provides us a picture of something separated from the whole by worry, resulting in a divided and fractured soul. Jesus tells us that this will literally "choke" the Word. He was describing a condition where we are cut off from His provision and life supply—effectively, a spiritually suffocated state.

We must be on guard against anything that pulls our attention away from the Word of God. Far too many Christians need to be made aware of these truths. They do not understand that our eyes and ears are the gateways to our souls. Everything we look at or listen to has the potential to plant either corruptible seeds or incorruptible seeds. I am including the television shows, movies, and newscasts we watch. Few realize that their favorite sitcoms may be the very thing that has led them to be cut off from the life of Jesus, effectively blocking His miraculous power from flowing into their lives.

How Committed Are You?

My spouse and I enjoy serving others, but we prioritize safeguarding the Word of God in our personal and family life. This applies to all acquaintances, even close friends and family members. Our relationship with God is paramount, and we are willing to sever ties with anyone who introduces corruptible seeds that may suffocate the incorruptible seeds in our hearts. We may interact with them in a church or ministry setting, but we will limit our association to protect our hearts.

How determined are you to protect the Word of God that has been sown in your heart? Satan will come at you with everything in his arsenal to steal it or introduce corruptible seeds capable of choking the life from it. He will use close friends, family members, coworkers, and others to pull you away from the Word. Once, in my life, he even used a pastor who tried to "counsel" me to not become overly extreme in my commitment to the Word!

The Cost Is High, but the Reward Is Higher

The cost is high to pursue revelation knowledge from Scripture, but the benefits far outweigh whatever price you will have to pay. Satan will make sure the road ahead is rough. However, once the Word begins to germinate and produce a harvest, it will be difficult for anyone to convince you to withdraw or turn back.

Peter tells us that God has provided "all things that pertain to life and godliness, through the knowledge of Him who called us" (2 Peter 1:3). He was referring to the revelation knowledge that we have been discussing. This knowledge grows from the incorruptible seeds planted in our hearts if we protect them and refuse to allow Satan or his demons to steal them.

Our ministry is experiencing incredible manifestations that we never imagined possible. This results from our unwavering commitment to pursuing the Word of God, no matter the cost. Our journey has been challenging, but today, my wife and I can look back and confidently say that everything the Lord has accomplished through us is worth every sacrifice we made.

As Paul encouraged Timothy, we, too, must "fight the good fight of faith" and "lay hold on eternal life" (1 Timothy 6:12). Jesus defined eternal life as a deep, intimate relationship with Him and our heavenly Father (John 17:3). While some may present the Christian life as easy and effortless, we know that there will be battles to fight. Our enemy understands the power of revelation knowledge and will do everything possible to prevent us from pursuing the Word of God and allowing it to take root in our hearts.

We Are Not Alone in the Battle

My goal is to open your eyes to the source of your problems. Satan is on the attack. Do not let yourself become overly focused on the people he uses. We must never forget he has blinded them, and most do not realize he is using them. Some will even think they speak for God, just like the pastor I referenced.

Jesus told His disciples that it would be advantageous for Him to leave them (John 16:7). His departure opened the door for the Holy Spirit to come. The Spirit now dwells in our spirit, and He will never leave us alone to fight our battles. He is standing by to help you with each step on your journey into the plan of God. All you have to do is ask for His help. You will find Him ready and waiting to give it.

Paul told Timothy to "fight the good fight of faith" and to "lay hold on eternal life." Jesus defined eternal life in John 17:3 as knowing God. Faith is grounded in the Word of God. Our ability to exercise faith directly relates to our relationship with God. You will find that He will always welcome you into His presence with arms open wide if you take that first step toward Him.

Chapter 21

Pursuing Deep Roots in God's Word through Meditation

"He who has ears to hear, let him hear!"
MATTHEW 13:9

People often use their phones during church services, while dining out, and even while driving. These distractions can take our focus away from the Word and prevent us from listening to the Spirit's voice. I often wonder how many Christians in my circle struggle with being fully present and attentive during these moments. We must retrain ourselves to filter out distractions and actively listen with a receptive mindset to hear what the Spirit of God is trying to communicate. If we neglect to do so, we may miss out on revelation knowledge and make ourselves vulnerable to Satan's attempts to steal the incorruptible seed planted in our hearts (Matthew 13:19).

Four Conditions of the Heart

Jesus describes four conditions of the heart in the parable of the sower. We discussed two of these in the last chapter. Each of the four represents a different level of receptiveness to God's Word. The first represents a person with no understanding of God's Word. We find Jesus' description of it in Mark 4:16–17:

> "These likewise are the ones sown on stony ground who, when they hear the word, immediately receive it with gladness; and they have no root in themselves, and so endure only for a time. Afterward, when tribulation or persecution arises for the word's sake, immediately they stumble."

I have met many Christians who are stuck in this place. They attend a service or listen to a message online and get excited by the revelation being released. Some will even robustly shout "Amen" at the preacher to show their agreement. They genuinely personify Jesus' description of the person who receives the Word with gladness.

Did you notice in verse 17 that Jesus described these people as having "no root in themselves"? The Greek word for "root" describes a person who has acquired knowledge but has not allowed it to penetrate deeply into the innermost parts of their soul.

Deeply Rooted in God's Word

The key to why God's Word does not produce fruit in our lives lies in this statement: "no root in themselves." I have already referenced the meaning of the Greek word for "root." The Greek word for "in" depicts something operating from the inside. Taken together, we see that Jesus spoke of a person who has not allowed His Words to penetrate deeply into the innermost parts of their soul. As the soul is the gateway between our spirit and the physical realm, the result will be that God's power will not be able to flow outward through our soul.

Many people get excited about the words of their favorite preacher and can even quote their teaching verbatim, yet they struggle to do the same with Scripture. However, it's important to remember that walking in someone else's revelation can be dangerous. For instance, a preacher once gave his car to a needy family because he felt led by the Spirit. As a result, he was blessed with a better car. However, many people who heard his testimony gave away their cars, expecting the same blessing, but it didn't happen. This is because the Spirit hadn't asked them to give away their cars, so they had no right to expect the same result.

God never intended for us to walk in another person's revelation. The Word of God is filled with incorruptible seeds that can only take root in our souls if we spend time meditating on them. There are no shortcuts to developing a deep understanding of the Word of God. You must put in the effort.

Do Not Let Satan Laugh at You

You must dig in and make the Word of God a part of you. It does not matter what I or any other minister may say. The devil will attack, and if you have not expended the effort to make the revelation yours, he will succeed in stealing the Word. You can quote your favorite minister and end up in the same situation as the seven sons of Sceva:

> Now God worked unusual miracles by the hands of Paul, so that even handkerchiefs or aprons were brought from his body to the sick, and the diseases left them and the evil spirits went out of them. Then some of the itinerant Jewish exorcists took it upon themselves to call the name of the Lord Jesus over those who had evil spirits, saying, "We exorcise you by the Jesus whom Paul preaches." Also there were seven sons of Sceva, a Jewish chief priest, who did so. And the evil spirit answered and said, "Jesus I know, and Paul I know; but who are you?" Then the man in whom the evil spirit was leaped on them, overpowered

them, and prevailed against them, so that they fled out of that house naked and wounded. (Acts 19:11–16)

The itinerant Jewish exorcists tried to cast out evil spirits, saying, "We exorcise you by the Jesus whom Paul preaches" (Acts 19:13). I picture the spirits laughing at the men as they jumped on them and began to beat them. You must never forget faith will not work in your life unless you first meditate on the Word to the point that you can confidently say from your spirit, "Thus saith the Lord." This will not happen until the Word is allowed to penetrate deeply into your soul, where it can produce a harvest of revelation knowledge.

Growing into Revelation Knowledge Like a Mustard Seed

If you are unfamiliar with these concepts, they might seem overwhelming. Don't allow fear to prevent you from committing time to meditate on the Word. Just like a farmer cannot plant a seed and immediately harvest corn, no one can instantly become deeply rooted in the Word. Developing a solid understanding takes time, much like how corn takes time to grow and mature. With patience, the Word will take root in your soul and produce a harvest of revelation knowledge, as Jesus explained in the parable of the mustard seed:

> Then He said, "To what shall we liken the kingdom of God? Or with what parable shall we picture it? It is like a mustard seed which, when it is sown on the ground, is smaller than all the seeds on earth; but when it is sown, it grows up and becomes greater than all herbs, and shoots out large branches, so that the birds of the air may nest under its shade." (Mark 4:30–32)

The mustard seed is the smallest of all seeds when first planted. It will grow taproots extending three to five feet deep in the ground before the first blade appears above the ground. From this foundation, it will then grow into a mighty tree that cannot easily be moved by any storm winds. Like the mustard seed, the seed of God's Word may seem small and insignificant when we begin to plant it. Over time it has the potential to grow deep roots that will produce a tree of revelation as mighty as the tree in Jesus' parable.

The Need for Patience

Many people begin to pursue the Word of God but become discouraged and give up at the first sign of adversity. However, impatience can hinder our ability to fully experience all God has planned for us. We must be patient to receive all that God has provided through Christ Jesus, as it takes time for the seed to take root and produce a harvest.

It's important to remember that time is needed for the seed to germinate and develop deep roots in our hearts. Many individuals pursue the vision God has given them, only to see their progress collapse at the slightest challenge. This is often because they lack deep roots in the Word.

Like many others, I began my Christian journey with excitement and a desire to serve God. However, my church did not emphasize the importance of developing deep roots in the Word. Instead, they encouraged new believers to minister immediately to the sick and hurting. I prayed for many people with minimal results. The constant push to minister without a solid grounding in the Word led to an almost continuous sense of discouragement.

Walking in Power Requires Us to First Meditate

Do you want to walk in the power and anointing of the Spirit? If your answer is yes, are you also willing to dig into God's Word and stay there until your mind is transformed? Those willing to do this will see the Holy Spirit's power flowing outward from their spirits as more and more of the Word seeds become deeply rooted in their hearts. It will take time and some late hours, but the reward for your efforts will be fruit that remains eternally.

Again, I am referring to our need to meditate on the Word of God. Meditation is often misunderstood in the church today. It means focusing consistently and constantly on a specific thing. Watching a television program or movie is an example of meditation. We sit for hours doing those things and complain about not having time for God's Word. Our enemy is not a lack of time but a lack of discipline in choosing what we will meditate on. All of us have the same amount of time. Some use it for meditation on news headlines, sporting events, or movies, while others use it on God's Word. Which will you choose?

God Uses All Who Will Pay the Price

I have studied the stories of influential figures in ministry, such as Smith Wigglesworth and Oral Roberts. These individuals witnessed remarkable displays of God's power during their gatherings, and I hoped to one day experience similar manifestations. However, my pastor told me these occurrences were only meant for those with a "special" calling from God. Through my studies, I have learned that he was mistaken. God intends for all His children to partake in the miraculous, but only a few are willing to pay the price to achieve it. After examining the lives of those whom God has used mightily,

I have noticed a common theme: these individuals chose to discipline themselves and pay the necessary price to ground themselves in God's Word firmly.

Oral Roberts is one such example. Oral Roberts became frustrated by the lack of power in his ministry in his early years. He read accounts of miraculous demonstrations in the four Gospels and the book of Acts but did not see the same things in his ministry. The Lord led him to read through the Gospels and the book of Acts three times consecutively on his knees. He did, and power followed. From that time of intentional seeking, God built an international ministry through which millions were brought to salvation.

There are many other examples of great men and women throughout church history whom God has used in remarkable ways, but I cannot discuss them all here. Dr. Roberts's experience is an excellent demonstration of how patience and dedication can lead to great rewards. Many people desire to witness the Holy Spirit's power, but only some are willing to pay the price. Although God may not require you to kneel for thirty days, there will be a price to pay. In a world where people seek immediate gratification, it's challenging to find individuals willing to exercise patience and devote time to become firmly grounded in God's Word.

The Storms Don't Affect Those with Deep Roots

We all desire to be used miraculously by God just as He used Jesus and the apostles. This will not happen if we do not give time to become deeply rooted in God's Word. How this happens will be different for each of us. The Holy Spirit led Oral Roberts to kneel for thirty days while reading through the Gospels and Acts. I was led to spend a certain number of hours in prayer while listening to Paul's letters being read through an audio Bible. One of my instructors in Bible school was led to stand on the edge of her bathtub while reading the Bible out loud for several months. How He leads you will be different but similar to these experiences. I cannot emphasize how important it is to not parrot what others have done. Allow the Holy Spirit to lead; you will know what to do.

I live with my family in Florida, and we have experienced several major hurricanes. I have observed that these storms easily knock down trees with shallow roots. I have seen massive oak trees lying on their sides with small root balls at their bases. You can follow the example of the mustard seed in Mark 4:30–32 and develop deep roots. This will give you a strong foundation, and even when the storms rage around you, you will not be uprooted like those vulnerable oak trees.

Chapter 22

Total Commitment to God's Word Provides Protection from the Storms

> *Another parable He put forth to them, saying: "The kingdom of heaven is like a mustard seed, which a man took and sowed in his field, which indeed is the least of all the seeds; but when it is grown it is greater than the herbs and becomes a tree, so that the birds of the air come and nest in its branches."*
>
> MATTHEW 13:31–32

It is important to develop a strong foundation in the Word of God. Satan has a plan to steal the Word from us, which can only be overcome with a deep and robust understanding of the Word. This is similar to trees in a storm—those with stronger and deeper roots are more likely to withstand the storm. While there is no guarantee that storms won't come, a strong foundation in the Word can help us stand firm when they pass.

The Fountain of Living Water

During a meeting with a Samaritan woman, Jesus discussed the living water that He provides His followers:

> Jesus answered and said to her, "Whoever drinks of this water will thirst again, but whoever drinks of the water that I shall give him will never thirst. But the water that I shall give him will become in him a fountain of water springing up into everlasting life." (John 4:13–14)

Throughout the previous chapters, we have extensively covered the topics of meditation and relationship. In John 4:13–14, Jesus mentioned the "fountain of water springing up into everlasting life." I have listened to numerous sermons about the living water Jesus spoke of. Some sermons focused on the Holy Spirit, while others emphasized meditating on Scripture or power flowing from our spirits. However, they all left me questioning how we can access this living water.

One day, the Spirit of God drew my attention to the Greek word for "everlasting." I learned it is the same Greek word used in John 17:3, where Jesus speaks of eternal life. In that verse, Jesus defines eternal life as knowing the only true God and Jesus Christ. The word translated as "know" is *ginosko*, which refers to knowledge gained through personal experience or firsthand acquaintance with someone.

Gaining firsthand experience with a person is only possible if you spend time with them. *Ginosko* is also seen in Mary's response to the angel Gabriel (Luke 1:34). Gabriel appeared to her with a message that she would give birth to the Messiah. She asked how this could be "since I do not *know* a man" (emphasis added). Mary was a virgin and had never been intimate with a man. She did not understand how she could conceive the promised child.

Drinking from the Well

Jesus' teaching on eternal life paints a picture of the close relationship that God desires to have with each of His children. The Greek word for "life" is *zoe*, which refers to a life that originates from and is sustained by God's self-existent life. Combining this with the word *eternal* gives us a glimpse of the kind of relationship we can have with God that allows us to draw from His life and be sustained by it.

We must cultivate intimacy with Jesus and our heavenly Father to access this living water. The enemy may try to make us feel unworthy. Still, we can be confident that God has chosen us to stand before Him, blameless and holy, through our faith in Jesus (Ephesians 1:4). This is possible because Jesus' sacrifice on the cross has washed away our sins and made us righteous before God. Only through Jesus' redemptive work can we approach God and experience the abundant life He offers.

We Live from Relationship, Not Experiences

During my early years serving Christ, I had the privilege of witnessing powerful movements of the Spirit. The church where I became a Christian experienced a revival that lasted for several years and attracted tens of thousands of visitors from around the globe. We celebrated the outpouring by shouting, dancing, and running every night. However, I struggled to grasp the concept of eternal life from our relationship with God.

In those early years, I attended many conferences and church meetings where emotions ran high. While I don't critique these experiences, I now understand that physical manifestations should not take precedence over the presence of the Holy Spirit. It's essential not to become "addicted" to these experiences.

In chapter 1, I shared my experience in a small country church. I attended that small church before the meetings where I experienced these manifestations. However, I forgot a crucial lesson I learned in that church and other small country churches over a two-year period: to prioritize the Holy Spirit as a person over what He can do for us.

While it's wonderful to have emotional encounters resulting from manifestations of His presence during services, it's even more valuable to spend quiet moments in fellowship with Him in our secret place. In my observation, many Christians are unaware of the level of intimacy they can have with the Holy Spirit.

Moving beyond Emotionalism

I believe most failures in the Christian life are rooted in our lack of intimacy with the Holy Spirit. Jesus referred to this as a state of having "no root in himself" (Matthew 13:21). In context, He was talking about the Word. Still, as I have said, it is impossible to experience intimacy with the Spirit separate from the Word of God. In *Thayer's Greek Lexicon*, the word translated as "root" in this verse means a person "who has but a superficial experience of divine truth and has not permitted it to make its way into the inmost recesses of the soul."[1]

I would shout and dance in the services mentioned, but I experienced no lasting change. Satan would wait at the door and immediately bombard my mind with thoughts of unworthiness and failure. My addiction to "the experience" over the presence of the Spirit led to an endless cycle of shouting, dancing, and condemnation. Thankfully, the Holy Spirit was patient and kept drawing me back to Himself. He helped me discover that my way out of the cycle was to develop deep roots in the Word of God in addition to spending time with Him.

Satan Longs to Devour Us

Many Christians have fallen into the same trap I did. They believe in God but seem to be in an endless cycle of emotional experiences with only minimal victory over Satan in their lives. They "believe" in God and think this is enough. James tells us that Satan and his

---

1. *Thayer's Greek Lexicon*, s.v. "rhiza," accessed July 11, 2023, https://biblehub.com/greek/4491.htm.

minions also believe in God (James 2:19). The difference between him and us is that we are invited into an intimate relationship with God. You were made worthy by the blood of Jesus to experience this.

We must give the Word of God time to penetrate the deepest recesses of our souls. We will not have confidence in our relationship with God until this happens. Peter tells us that Satan is on the prowl "like a roaring lion" looking for Christians who will open the door for him to devour them (1 Peter 5:8). Jesus told His disciples that those who have no "root" in His Word will fall into Satan's trap and be led into destruction when they experience any level of "tribulation or persecution" because of their relationship with God and His Word (Matthew 13:21).

We see in Matthew 13:57 that Jesus' ministry offended His family. Interestingly, the same Greek word is found in verse 21 as "immediately he stumbles." Satan set a trap utilizing family connection, and Jesus' family fell into it. How would you react if your family criticized you for believing God could heal you? If you had not allowed the Word to develop deep roots in your soul, you would be positioned to fall into Satan's trap by allowing yourself to be hurt or upset by their criticism.

Taking Thoughts Captive

I have heard many messages over the years focused on spiritual warfare. Most were concentrated outwardly on Satan's work in our lives, families, or even cities and regions. Paul took a different approach in his second letter to the Corinthian believers.

> For though we walk in the flesh, we do not war according to the flesh. For the weapons of our warfare *are* not carnal but mighty in God for pulling down strongholds, casting down arguments and every high thing that exalts itself

against the knowledge of God, bringing every thought into captivity to the obedience of Christ, and being ready to punish all disobedience when your obedience is fulfilled. (2 Corinthians 10:3–6)

The traps Satan uses to cause us to fall are all focused on our souls. They take the form of thoughts such as, "Why would they say that about you?" You can choose to accept the thoughts or reject them. Paul refers to this as "bringing every thought into captivity" (2 Corinthians 10:5).

In verse 5, Paul tells us the target of Satan's attack is "the knowledge of God." He is referring to the Word of God, but there is more to Satan's attack than causing us to question Scripture. HELPS Word-Studies tells us the specific knowledge Paul refers to is "functional ('working') knowledge gleaned from first-hand (personal) experience."[2] This type of knowledge can only be considered as accurate as the relationship from which it came. In other words, Satan will work to insert thoughts that cause us to question Scripture and God Himself to interrupt our relationship with Him.

Throughout the years, I've received cautionary advice from ministers about being overly focused on the Word. They suggested I find balance in my life and even recommended watching sitcoms and movies to stay "relevant." However, I disagree. Becoming too established in your relationship with God and His Word is impossible. Jesus spent entire nights in prayer, John the Baptist spent thirty years in the desert, and Paul spent three years in the desert of Arabia outside of Damascus. Although many sermons discuss their ministries, few mention the time each spent becoming grounded in the Word of God.

---

2. HELPS Word-Studies, s.v. "gnósis," accessed July 11, 2023, https://biblehub.com/greek/1108.htm.

Chapter 23

Press into God's Love by Praying in the Spirit

Beloved, let us love one another, for love is of God; and everyone who loves is born of God and knows God. He who does not love does not know God, for God is love. In this the love of God was manifested toward us, that God has sent His only begotten Son into the world, that we might live through Him. In this is love, not that we loved God, but that He loved us and sent His Son to be the propitiation for our sins. Beloved, if God so loved us, we also ought to love one another.

1 JOHN 4:7–11

Two main themes have emerged throughout our discussion: cultivating a close relationship with God and dedicating time to daily meditation on His Word. These two are intertwined and essential to obtaining revelation knowledge. Without a strong relationship with God, one cannot move beyond a surface-level understanding of Scripture and will be in danger of falling into religious tradition. In this chapter, we will focus specifically on how to develop and strengthen our relationship with God.

God Is Love

According to John, "God is love." If someone is not practicing love, they cannot honestly "know" God (1 John 4:8). The word *know* is also used in John 17:3 and 2 Corinthians 10:5. It refers to a kind of knowledge acquired through personal experience with someone. It's important to note that John uses the words *does not* to negate the word *know* in 1 John 4:8. This tells us that those who don't practice love cannot have a personal experience with God, which is necessary for building a close relationship with Him.

Christians often face challenges and difficulties in their spiritual journey because they lack a deep connection with God. We may have learned about Him from others, Bible studies, or church services, but few of us set aside time to spend with Him personally. Just like human relationships, intimacy with God requires intentional time spent in His presence.

You Can Intentionally Cultivate God's Love

To truly understand God, we must cultivate love. But how do we go about doing this? Can we intentionally cultivate love, or is it something that happens by chance? Jude provides us with the answer to this question.

> But you, beloved, building yourselves up on your most holy faith, praying in the Holy Spirit, keep yourselves in the love of God, looking for the mercy of our Lord Jesus Christ unto eternal life. (Jude 1:20–21)

According to Jude, praying in the Spirit can strengthen our faith. However, many teachings on this topic only focus on verse 20 and overlook verse 21. In verse 21, Jude explains that praying in the Spirit can also help us stay in God's love. This is one of the significant benefits of praying in the Spirit.

Some people have asked me to pray for God to pour His love into them. But verse 21 reminds us that walking in God's love is our responsibility. Praying in the Spirit can help us yield to God's love and experience it more fully. Jude also tells us that this type of prayer is how we "keep" ourselves in the love of God.

Ultimately, we can determine the level of our experience with God's love. If you feel like you're not experiencing it enough, try praying more in the Spirit. Unfortunately, many people focus too much on their physical senses and miss the joy of experiencing God's love in their lives.

God Has Already Supplied What We Need

Many Christians struggle with depression and discouragement, often feeling little joy in their spiritual journeys. They may seek prayer for relief at church altars. As someone who used to experience this, I found guidance in 2 Peter 1:2–4 through the Holy Spirit.

> Grace and peace be multiplied to you in the knowledge of God and of Jesus our Lord, as His divine power has given to us all things that *pertain* to life and godliness, through the knowledge of Him who called us by glory and virtue, by which have been given to us exceedingly great and precious promises, that through these you may be partakers of the divine nature, having escaped the corruption *that is* in the world through lust.

I discovered a sense of freedom through these Bible verses. According to Peter, knowledge of God leads to an increase of "grace and peace" in our lives. He was not referring to acquired knowledge. Therefore, if we lack peace, it is likely due to a lack of revelation knowledge we receive from the Spirit while meditating on Scripture.

In Galatians 5:22–23, Paul talks about the qualities that should be evident in every Christian, including "love," "joy," and "peace." If we are not experiencing these qualities, it may be because we are not maintaining our relationship with God. Instead of asking Him for something we already have, we should focus on deepening our relationship with Him through prayer and time with the Holy Spirit. The more we do this, the more we will experience His love, which is where we will find Him.

While reading these words, some may experience feelings of condemnation. However, Paul reminds us that we can use the Word of God to take negative feelings captive. Training ourselves to consistently respond to negative thoughts with God's promises is important.

Choosing to Walk in His Love

In the book of Romans, Paul explains that the Holy Spirit has already poured out the love of God into our hearts (Romans 5:5). We do not have to wait for it; His love already exists within us. To learn how to walk in this love, we can look to Jude 1:21 for guidance:

> Keep yourselves in the love of God, looking for the mercy of our Lord Jesus Christ unto eternal life.

In this verse, "you" are the implied subject. God has given us the power to choose the level of His love that we want to experience. If you pray in the Spirit, you will notice that His love becomes more apparent. If you are not familiar with this type of prayer, don't worry. We will discuss it in more detail in the next chapter.

Yielding to the Spirit in Prayer

At the altar, many people have asked me to pray for "a baptism of love." However, they don't realize that if they have already accepted Jesus as their Lord, then love Himself lives within them. According to John, we are born of God and experience His love because "God is love" (1 John 4:8). Instead of seeking a baptism of love, we should seek a revelation of this love from the Holy Spirit.

God has given us His Spirit and the ability to pray as He guides us (Acts 2:4). By dedicating time to prayer, we can increase our awareness of God's presence. At first, our flesh and soul may resist this change because they are no longer the center of our lives. But prayer will become easier as we continue to yield to the Spirit.

It's important to keep in mind that God isn't responsible for making us aware of His love. Instead, He's provided us with His Spirit to assist us in our prayers. In Jude 1:21, we're reminded to "keep [ourselves] in the love of God" by praying in the Spirit. The Holy Spirit is ready and willing to aid us in our prayers, but it's up to us to invite Him. Sadly, many people don't ask for His help. However, I believe you will ask for His help, and as a result, He will guide you toward an experience of God's love that is beyond your imagination.

Chapter 24

Press into Revelation Knowledge by Praying in the Spirit

Then, the same day at evening, being the first day of the week, when the doors were shut where the disciples were assembled, for fear of the Jews, Jesus came and stood in the midst, and said to them, "Peace be with you." When He had said this, He showed them His hands and His side. Then the disciples were glad when they saw the Lord. So Jesus said to them again, "Peace to you! As the Father has sent Me, I also send you." And when He had said this, He breathed on them, and said to them, "Receive the Holy Spirit. If you forgive the sins of any, they are forgiven them; if you retain the sins of any, they are retained."

JOHN 20:19–23

It is important to have a clear understanding of speaking with tongues. Unfortunately, many people who have received the "baptism in the Holy Spirit" have not been adequately taught about this experience. As mentioned in the previous chapter, the associated prayer language is crucial for deepening our connection with God's love. In this chapter, we will look at how speaking in tongues can help us uncover revelation knowledge from our spirits, much like drawing water from a well using a bucket.

You Do Not Have to Speak in Tongues

There is a misconception among some people that speaking in tongues is a requirement to be a Christian. However, this is not true. According to John 20:22, Jesus breathed on His disciples and told them to receive the Holy Spirit. The original Greek text says that He "breathed into" them, and at that moment, the Holy Spirit entered their spirits, and they were spiritually reborn. In Acts, Jesus instructed His disciples to wait for the baptism of the Holy Spirit, despite having already received the Spirit when Jesus breathed into them. The reason for this is explained in Acts 1:8:

> "But you shall receive power *when the Holy Spirit has come upon you*; and you shall be witnesses to Me in Jerusalem, and in all Judea and Samaria, and to the end of the earth." (Emphasis added)

The phrase "upon you" is crucial for understanding why Jesus instructed His followers to wait for the Holy Spirit before becoming witnesses. When we accept Jesus as our Lord, the Holy Spirit enters our spirit, which we often refer to as salvation or being born again. However, Jesus referred to a second experience beyond salvation in Acts 1, where the Spirit empowered the disciples with anointing. This is commonly known as the baptism of the Spirit. The prayer language mentioned earlier is associated with this experience.

The Spirit Provides Utterance and We Speak

The disciples waited in the upper room as instructed by Jesus until the Holy Spirit was poured out on the day of Pentecost:

> When the Day of Pentecost had fully come, they were all with one accord in one place. And suddenly there

came a sound from heaven, as of a rushing mighty wind, and it filled the whole house where they were sitting. Then there appeared to them divided tongues, as of fire, and one sat upon each of them. And they were all filled with the Holy Spirit and began to speak with other tongues, as the Spirit gave them utterance. (Acts 2:1–4)

In Acts 2, the disciples were following Jesus' instruction to wait as they sat praying in the upper room on the day of Pentecost. Suddenly, a sound filled the house, and they were filled with the Spirit. They spoke with other tongues as the Spirit gave them utterance, but the Spirit did not take control of their tongues. Each person had to yield their own tongue and speak the utterance provided. This practice has not changed in the past two thousand years. The Spirit will provide you with the utterance, but you must open your mouth and speak, just as the disciples did.

If these things are new to you, I recommend you ask the Holy Spirit to teach you and dedicate some time to quietly wait for Him, following Jesus' advice to His disciples. He will meet you wherever you are and guide you through each step, just as He has done with countless Christians since the day of Pentecost over two thousand years ago.

In the previous chapter, I talked about the importance of praying in the Spirit to stay connected to God's love, as mentioned in Jude 1:21. If you spend more time praying with the guidance of the Holy Spirit, you'll experience a greater manifestation of His love. However, some readers may not be familiar with this type of prayer, so I've provided more details about it at the beginning of this chapter. The remainder of this chapter will explore how we can access revelation knowledge by dedicating time to praying in the Spirit.

Prophecy and Tongues

In 1 Corinthians 14:2–4, Paul offers further guidance on praying in tongues and prophecy. These practices are linked to accessing God's wisdom.

> For he who speaks in a tongue does not speak to men but to God, for no one understands him; however, in the spirit he speaks mysteries. But he who prophesies speaks edification and exhortation and comfort to men. He who speaks in a tongue edifies himself, but he who prophesies edifies the church.

These verses emphasize that prophecy is the most valuable gift for public gatherings. It can benefit everyone if it is delivered accurately and aligns with biblical teachings. Although many individuals claim to be prophets nowadays, their messages often contradict Scripture. We must reject all prophecies that do not align with the Word of God.

Accessing Revelation Knowledge

Lately, I have been praying more in tongues than in English because it helps me strengthen my faith and minister strength to myself. Praying in the Spirit and meditating on God's Word helps me gain revelation knowledge in a more profound way.

Revelation knowledge is different from academic knowledge that we gain from schools. It is the knowledge that we acquire from the Spirit of God. Unlike intellectual knowledge, which we force ourselves to learn, revelation knowledge comes to us naturally. We use acquired knowledge every day, whether we are driving our cars, completing work or school assignments, or doing other tasks.

According to John, we as Christians possess an anointing from the Holy One, which grants us the ability to know all things (1 John

2:20). This type of knowledge, which I call revelation knowledge, is unique to believers and cannot be gained through academic studies or books. Through the Holy Spirit, Christians can be supernaturally given this knowledge. It is important to note that all Christians have access to this anointing mentioned by John.

Revelation Knowledge Is Available to Every Christian

Paul received the gospel he preached through a revelation from Jesus Christ (Galatians 1:11–12). John notes that we also have access to the same source of knowledge that Paul had.

> But the anointing which you have received from Him abides in you, and you do not need that anyone teach you; but as the same anointing teaches you concerning all things, and is true, and is not a lie, and just as it has taught you, you will abide in Him. (1 John 2:27)

To receive the revelation Paul and John wrote about, self-effort or academic studies completed in Bible college or seminary are not enough. This revelation can only be accessed through personal fellowship with the Spirit of God, which involves praying in tongues and meditating on Scripture. By prioritizing these practices in our daily routines, we can elevate our way of living to a much higher level.

People Were Amazed and Offended by Jesus' Teachings

Jesus ministered from the revelation knowledge God taught Him (John 8:28). How many of us can say, like Jesus, that we only teach the things taught to us by the Spirit? Can you imagine the impact we would have if this were true? Mark tells us that people were "astonished" by Jesus' messages:

> And when the Sabbath had come, He began to teach in the synagogue. And many hearing *Him* were astonished, saying, "Where *did* this Man *get* these things? And what wisdom *is* this which is given to Him, that such mighty works are performed by His hands!" (Mark 6:2)

Observe how people reacted to the messages delivered by Jesus. He only spoke what His heavenly Father taught, which was clear to everyone who listened. However, some were offended because they only saw Him as the boy from the neighborhood who had grown up in a carpenter's shop:

> And the Jews marveled, saying, "How does this Man know letters, having never studied?" Jesus answered them and said, "My doctrine is not Mine, but His who sent Me. If anyone wills to do His will, he shall know concerning the doctrine, whether it is from God or *whether* I speak on My own *authority.*" (John 7:15–17)

Jesus received divine revelation from God and shared it with the people. He operated on a higher level than the educated individuals of His time. Fortunately, we, too, can access the same knowledge by regularly seeking the guidance of the Holy Spirit and studying God's Word.

The Holy Spirit Is Our Teacher

We do not have evidence of any old covenant teacher praying in tongues. There is also no evidence that Jesus did. The gift of tongues did not manifest before Pentecost when the Holy Spirit was poured out on the followers of Christ meeting in the upper room (Acts 2:1–4).

In John 14:25–26, Jesus promised His disciples that the Holy Spirit would teach them everything and remind them of everything He had said to them. Jesus Himself was taught by the Father (John 8:28). Now the Holy Spirit works in our lives to reveal the same revelation that Jesus received.

> But God has revealed them to us through His Spirit. For the Spirit searches all things, yes, the deep things of God. For what man knows the things of a man except the spirit of the man which is in him? Even so no one knows the things of God except the Spirit of God. Now we have received, not the spirit of the world, but the Spirit who is from God, that we might know the things that have been freely given to us by God. (1 Corinthians 2:10–12)

In 1 Corinthians 14:2, Paul provides insight into how one can receive revelation knowledge from the Spirit. He explains that the one who prays in tongues "speaks mysteries." As someone who wrote nearly two-thirds of the New Testament, Paul informed the Galatian readers that his teachings and writings were obtained through the "revelation of Jesus Christ" (Galatians 1:12). We will delve deeper into this topic in the following chapter, but I'd like to leave you with one final thought to contemplate. Paul informed the Corinthian believers that he spoke in tongues more frequently than they did (1 Corinthians 14:18), which is why he attained a higher level of revelation knowledge.

Chapter 25

Are We Relying on Acquired or Revelation Knowledge?

For he who speaks in a tongue does not speak to men but to God, for no one understands him; however, in the spirit he speaks mysteries.

1 CORINTHIANS 14:2

I magine accessing God's knowledge and receiving answers to all your problems. This is how God wants every Christian to live. To achieve this, pray from your spirit while being open to the guidance of the Holy Spirit. This type of prayer helps us tap into God's knowledge and understand things that may have seemed like mysteries before. It's the "hidden wisdom" that Paul talked about in 1 Corinthians 2:6–8:

> However, *we speak wisdom* among those who are mature, yet not the wisdom of this age, nor of the rulers of this age, who are coming to nothing. But *we speak the wisdom* of God in a mystery, the hidden *wisdom* which God ordained before the ages for our glory, which none of the rulers of this age knew; for had they known, they would not have crucified the Lord of glory. (Emphasis added)

It is entirely up to you to decide if you want to walk in revelation. God has given you His Spirit and Word, which provide you with everything you need to access His supernatural knowledge. The decision to focus your attention on the Word and yield to the Holy Spirit in prayer or to allow yourself to be distracted by the world around you is yours alone to make.

Will You Pursue God's Word Until It Becomes Revelation?

As a Christian, pursuing God's Word until it becomes a revelation is the most crucial decision you can make. A true understanding of God's Word will reveal His plan and purpose for your life.

You may have never experienced the amazing feeling of gaining revelation knowledge from praying in the Spirit. This can bring Scripture to life in ways you couldn't have imagined, making previously challenging texts crystal clear. It's difficult to describe, but there's nothing more exhilarating than having a moment of revelation.

While many Christians pray for outpourings of the Spirit and a modern-day revival, I've personally experienced these. I can confidently say that gaining a true revelation of God's Word is more valuable. Revivals are temporary, but understanding God's Word will empower you for a lifetime.

Paul's Example

Paul's writings demonstrate his reliance on revelation rather than acquired knowledge. In his first letter to the Corinthians, he wrote:

> And I, brethren, when I came to you, did not come with excellence of speech or of wisdom declaring to you the testimony of God. For I determined not to know anything

among you except Jesus Christ and Him crucified. I was with you in weakness, in fear, and in much trembling. And my speech and my preaching were not with persuasive words of human wisdom, but in demonstration of the Spirit and of power, that your faith should not be in the wisdom of men but in the power of God. (1 Corinthians 2:1–5)

Paul received what in modern times would be considered an Ivy League education from esteemed teachers. Despite his potential to impress with scholarly sermons, Paul chose to rely on the anointing of the Spirit of God to convey the gospel message. His trust in the Spirit's anointing resulted in miraculous demonstrations wherever he ministered. We see this further illustrated in chapter 4 of the same letter:

Now some are puffed up, as though I were not coming to you. But I will come to you shortly, if the Lord wills, and I will know, not the word of those who are puffed up, but the power. For the kingdom of God *is* not in word but in power. (1 Corinthians 4:18–20)

Paul was the first to bring the Corinthian believers to Christ, but after him, other ministers came and caused divisions among them, which is similar to our denominations in the church today. Paul was upset by this and sent Timothy to remind the Corinthians about the teachings of Christ that he had shared with them (1 Corinthians 4:17). We should never forget that our responsibility is to share God's Word, not the doctrines of any particular denomination. Paul gives us a further understanding of the message he preached:

However, we speak wisdom among those who are mature, yet not the wisdom of this age, nor of the rulers of this age,

who are coming to nothing. But we speak the wisdom of
God in a mystery, the hidden wisdom which God ordained
before the ages for our glory. (1 Corinthians 2:6–7)

The wisdom Paul describes in these verses is revelation knowledge, directly imparted into our spirit by the Holy Spirit as we meditate on the Word and fellowship with Him. Unfortunately, we have replaced this with intellectualism based solely on our acquired knowledge. Instead of relying on the Spirit, we have regressed to using our intellect.

The book of Acts shows that we are not impacting culture as effectively as the early church did. For instance, Peter, an uneducated fisherman, preached the first sermon and saw "about three souls" converted (Acts 2:41). Stephen, a deacon and the first church martyr, was "full of faith and power" and "did great wonders and signs among the people" (Acts 6:8). Although there is no indication that either Peter or Stephen received an education, they still performed miraculous acts just as Paul did.

Revelation Knowledge Is Available to You

But as it is written:

"Eye has not seen, nor ear heard,
Nor have entered into the heart of man
The things which God has prepared for those
who love Him."

But God has revealed them to us through His Spirit.
For the Spirit searches all things, yes, the deep things
of God. (1 Corinthians 2:9–10)

I've noticed that some ministers use verse 9 to argue that we can never understand God's ways. However, they seem to miss that Paul was quoting from the Old Testament (Isaiah 64:4), and in verse 10, he makes it clear that these things have now been revealed to us "through His Spirit."

Paul emphasized that we cannot rely solely on acquired knowledge to comprehend God's ways. Paul was highly educated, just like our modern-day seminary graduates. However, he didn't rely on his education, as some ministers do today. We have built institutions of learning that are void of the Spirit. I have met many men and women with seminary degrees who said they learned the Bible was not absolute truth during their educational pursuits. Our churches are full of people who have filled their heads with theological terminology but lack the presence of the Spirit of God.

Moving beyond Acquired Knowledge into Power

To minister effectively, we must go beyond academic studies and make time each day to develop our relationship with the Holy Spirit. Jesus sent the Holy Spirit to reveal God's ways to us. Still, many only see Him as a mysterious force that shows up during services. However, the Holy Spirit is ready to teach us if we are willing to recognize His presence. Unfortunately, many are unaware of His existence and miss out on His guidance, going from one difficulty to another without realizing the help they have access to in Him.

In 1 Corinthians 2:7, Paul talks about the wisdom of God that was once hidden but is now known to the church. This wisdom was a mystery to humanity before Christ, and even the Old Testament saints couldn't fully understand it. In 1 Corinthians 14:12, Paul sheds more light on how we can access this wisdom:

For he who speaks in a tongue does not speak to men but to God, for no one understands *him;* however, in the spirit he speaks mysteries.

In 1 Corinthians 2:7, Paul revealed that he spoke God's "hidden wisdom." How did he do this? I believe the answer is found in 1 Corinthians 14:2 where we see a person speaking in "tongues" is speaking "mysteries." HELPS Word-Studies tells us that these mysteries are "what can only be known through revelation."[3] We, too, can tap into this hidden wisdom by following Paul's example in prayer. As shown in Acts 2:4, the Holy Spirit will provide the words, but we must be willing to speak them. If this is new to you, take some time to listen quietly and let the Holy Spirit guide you step by step.

---

3. HELPS Word-Studies, s.v. "mustérion," accessed July 11, 2023, https://biblehub.com/greek/3466.htm.

Chapter 26

Accessing the Mind of Christ through the Holy Spirit

But when it pleased God, who separated me from my mother's womb and called me through His grace, to reveal His Son in me, that I might preach Him among the Gentiles, I did not immediately confer with flesh and blood, nor did I go up to Jerusalem to those who were apostles before me; but I went to Arabia, and returned again to Damascus. Then after three years I went up to Jerusalem to see Peter, and remained with him fifteen days. But I saw none of the other apostles except James, the Lord's brother. (Now concerning the things which I write to you, indeed, before God, I do not lie.)

GALATIANS 1:15–20

Saul was on his way to capture Christians and take them to Jerusalem for trial when he unexpectedly encountered Jesus on the road to Damascus. Although he wasn't seeking the Lord, Jesus had other plans. The encounter left Saul temporarily blind, and he had to be guided into Damascus. For three days he fasted and prayed, and his conversion likely occurred during this time.

The Lord then appeared to a disciple named Ananias in Damascus and instructed him to visit Saul and pray for him. Upon Ananias's prayer, Saul's vision was restored, and he was filled with the Holy Spirit (Acts 9:17–18).

Paul's Desert Experience

According to the Bible, Paul spent a few days in Damascus before traveling to Arabia (Acts 9:20–22). It is unclear how far south into the deserts of Arabia he journeyed, but we know that he eventually returned to Damascus. After three years, he went back to Jerusalem, as mentioned in Galatians 1:18. This visit was likely for consultation with the disciples.

After his conversion, Paul spent at least three years in Arabia, possibly in isolation, to deepen his connection with God. He mentioned speaking in tongues in 1 Corinthians 14:18 and expressed gratitude that he was able to do so more frequently than the believers in Corinth. My interpretation is that his time in the desert was spent praying out the mystery of the revelation of Jesus Christ mentioned in Galatians 1:11–12:

> But I make known to you, brethren, that the gospel which was preached by me is not according to man. For I neither received it from man, nor was I taught *it*, but *it came through the revelation of Jesus Christ*. (Emphasis added)

Paul spent at least three years in Arabia after his conversion. During this time, he may have lived as a hermit, trying to reconcile his new identity as a follower of Jesus with his previous persecution of the church. However, according to Acts 9:22, he also preached in Damascus and proved that Jesus was the Christ to the Jews. He likely began his ministry to the Gentiles after these three years.

Accessing the Wisdom of God

In 1 Corinthians 14:2, Paul states that we are speaking "mysteries" while praying in tongues. The term *mysteries* refers to knowledge that can only be revealed through revelation. This is the same term Paul used in 1 Corinthians 2:7–8:

> But *we speak the wisdom of God in a mystery*, the hidden *wisdom* which God ordained before the ages for our glory, which none of the rulers of this age knew; for had they known, they would not have crucified the Lord of glory. (Emphasis added)

I believe Paul spent much of his time in Arabia praying out the mystery of the "revelation of Jesus Christ" (Galatians 1:12). This revelation is also likely the "hidden wisdom" he spoke of in 1 Corinthians 2:7. It is hidden from the world but available to any Christians who will follow the example of Paul and separate themselves to seek it.

The Mind of Christ

Paul referenced "the mind of Christ" in 1 Corinthians 2:16. The word *mind* refers to the ability to receive God's thoughts. I do not believe Paul was telling his readers that their natural minds could access God's thoughts. Rather, our born again spirit has the ability to do this. This is where the gift of tongues comes into play, as it allows us to bypass our natural minds and pray straight from our spirits.

The Spirit of God sealed you in Christ after you heard "the gospel of your salvation" (Ephesians 1:13). According to 2 Corinthians 5:17, those who are "in Christ" become "a new creation" at that moment. Your spirit has been recreated and no longer has a sin nature; now you have access to God's presence and all the wisdom of heaven. John tells us that we now have an anointing imparted by the Holy Spirit that enables us to "know all things" (1 John 2:20). The original language refers to a gateway being opened from the spiritual realms that enables us to grasp spiritual truth with our natural wisdom. I believe this is what Paul spoke of when he encouraged his readers to pray for the ability to interpret what they spoke in tongues (1 Corinthians 14:13). Interpretation enables us to understand the revelation that was spoken while praying in tongues.

The Tongue Is Your Bucket

According to 1 Corinthians 14:14, when we speak in tongues, our spirit is doing the praying. By engaging in this practice, we are able to tap into God's secret wisdom, much like drawing water from a well with a bucket. Our tongue serves as the bucket we allow the Holy Spirit to use to communicate His teachings. This means that we have the ability to intentionally seek out divine wisdom for any challenge we may encounter.

You do not have to lean on your natural understanding. Jesus even told His disciples that the Holy Spirit would show them "things to come" (John 16:13). We can prepare for any situation by committing time to pray in tongues each day in partnership with the Holy Spirit. As we do this each day, answers to our questions will come. The Spirit communicates His answers in many ways, such as through a thought or idea that would never have come without His help.

An Example of His Protection Received in Prayer

A few years back, I felt an urge to pray in tongues before starting my day. I followed this prompting from the Spirit and prayed for about an hour before getting ready for the day. Although I didn't know why I was praying, it felt right, given that I had to speak at a recovery center later that evening.

As the day progressed, a few unexpected things came up, which caused me to leave home later than planned. I was anxious about being late for the meeting and hurried to get there. To reach the recovery center, I needed to turn right onto a four-lane highway that bordered our neighborhood. However, as I approached the intersection, I felt a strong urge to turn left, which would make me even later for the meeting.

Having spent enough time with the Holy Spirit, I recognized His prompting and obeyed. As I got in the left turn lane, the traffic light turned green, but the left turn lane had a red arrow. I stopped to wait, and a car behind me turned right on the green light. A vehicle approaching the intersection from the other direction didn't stop at their red light and collided with the car that had been behind me. If I had ignored the urging of the Spirit and turned right, I would have been in that accident. The Spirit later showed me that I had accessed His wisdom, leading me to recognize His promptings during my time of prayer in the morning.

Have you ever felt overwhelmed and unsure of what to do? I have found that the reason for this is often because we need to seek wisdom from the Spirit through prayer and believe in His guidance. I personally experienced the protection of the Spirit when I followed His prompting to pray and turn left instead of right. You, too, can invite the Spirit to lead you in prayer, and you can learn to recognize His guidance, but it will require time and effort. So, are you willing to do whatever it takes to pursue Him? Remember, the Spirit does not play favorites and is ready to lead you just as He led me. He will teach you to draw from God's hidden wisdom, and you will find yourself walking in higher and higher levels of His presence as you spend time each day with Him and begin to access the mind of Christ we have discussed in this chapter.

Chapter 27

Partnering with the Holy Spirit in Prayer to Draw from His Well of Perfect Knowledge

Likewise the Spirit also helps in our weaknesses. For we do not know what we should pray for as we ought, but the Spirit Himself makes intercession for us with groanings which cannot be uttered.

ROMANS 8:26

Most Christians I have met live their lives similarly to nonbelievers. They face the same health, financial, and mental challenges. Unfortunately, some churches teach that this is God's plan for their lives and that we can only find freedom in heaven. However, God has so much more in store for us. Through Christ Jesus, we can live a blessed life and have His Spirit guide us toward all the blessings He has prepared for us.

The Spirit Will Help Us Pray

Living a life of serving God should not mean struggling through the same challenges as those who do not. In the previous chapter, we learned about accessing the "mind of Christ" from 1 Corinthians 2:16, which provides wisdom and understanding for those who seek it. In Romans 8:26, Paul explains that the Holy Spirit helps us pray for things we might not even be aware of. Additionally, 1 Corinthians 14:2 and 14 highlight that praying in tongues allows our spirit to access the mysteries of God's hidden wisdom. We discussed this in the last chapter.

Spirit, Soul, and Body

Paul references the three parts of our being in 1 Thessalonians 5:23:

> Now may the God of peace Himself sanctify you completely; and *may your whole spirit, soul, and body* be preserved blameless at the coming of our Lord Jesus Christ. (Emphasis added)

I have heard ministers refer to the body as our "earth suit." It is left behind when we pass away and depart for our heavenly destination. When my father passed away years ago, the Lord allowed me to be with him on his arrival in heaven. We only have space to go through part of the experience in this book. He looked incredible and appeared to be in his late twenties or thirties. I had only ever known him physically, so seeing him looking so well was surprising. In the following weeks, the Holy Spirit reminded me of 2 Corinthians 5:17, which says:

> Therefore, if anyone is in Christ, he is a new creation; old things have passed away; behold, all things have become new.

At first, I believed my father had undergone a transformation when he passed away. However, the Holy Spirit revealed to me that we all experience spiritual change and become a new creation when we make Jesus the Lord of our life. During my time in heaven, I encountered my father's reborn spirit, which had previously inhabited his physical body.

Have you ever wondered about the difference between our spirit and soul? The soul is where our mind, will, intellect, and emotions reside, and it is often referred to as the heart. To help illustrate this concept, let's think about an egg. From the outside, an egg appears to be a single entity, but once cracked open, it reveals two distinct parts—the yolk and the white. Similarly, our heart consists of two parts—the soul and the spirit. According to Hebrews 4:12, the Word of God is the tool that can distinguish between the two:

> For the word of God is living and powerful, and sharper than any two-edged sword, piercing even to the division of soul and spirit, and of joints and marrow, and is a discerner of the thoughts and intents of the heart.

Some individuals have expressed their desire to move the Word of God from their mind to their spirit. However, they may not realize that the mind of Christ resides in the spirit. As explained earlier, we sow the incorruptible seed of God's Word (1 Peter 1:23) into our souls for renewal (Romans 12:2), leading to positive changes in our lives. We can then extract divine wisdom from our spirit, like drawing water from a well.

The Salvation of the Soul

When we make Jesus the Lord of our lives, the mind of Christ is deposited in our spirits. This provides us with spiritual knowledge that helps us renew our minds, which Paul talked about in Romans 12:2. James also encouraged his readers to accept "with meekness the implanted word, which is able to save your souls" (James 1:21). Although our spirits were recreated during salvation, we need to "plant" the Word of God in our souls. This allows the supernatural life in our spirits to flow freely through our souls into the physical realm. If we don't unclog our souls with God's incorruptible seed, it's like having a clot in an artery that starves the brain of oxygen, leading to a stroke. Death can continue working in our lives if we don't take care of our souls by feeding them a continuous stream of God's incorruptible Word seed.

The Dangers of an Unrenewed Mind

Since accepting Jesus and the Holy Spirit's residence in my spirit, I believe God's life is present in me. I often pray in tongues to ensure I am praying according to God's will. Our minds can be influenced by our carnal nature, which is why relying solely on them as a vehicle for prayer is problematic.

Sometimes our human nature can affect our prayer lives by causing us to pray with pride. I attended an all-night men's prayer meeting at my church when I was young. We were all determined to pray through the night in the sanctuary. However, I fell asleep immediately after kneeling to pray. Unbeknownst to the men around me, I slept through the entire night while kneeling. Everyone was impressed with my "prayer stamina" the next morning, but I struggled to admit the truth that I had been asleep.

> "But whatever city you enter, and they do not receive you, go out into its streets and say, 'The very dust of your city which clings to us we wipe off against you. Nevertheless know this, that the kingdom of God has come near you.' But I say to you that it will be more tolerable in that Day for Sodom than for that city. Woe to you, Chorazin! Woe to you, Bethsaida! For if the mighty works which were done in you had been done in Tyre and Sidon, they

would have repented long ago, sitting in sackcloth and ashes. But it will be more tolerable for Tyre and Sidon at the judgment than for you." (Luke 10:10–14)

A lot of individuals pray like the Pharisees mentioned in Luke. They depend only on their acquired knowledge and do not first renew their souls with God's Word. Paul tells us we can pray in the Spirit by using our understanding and spirits. But this can only happen if we first renew our minds with God's Word. Otherwise, our prayers will be prideful and founded on acquired knowledge.

Accessing God's Wisdom in Your Daily Life

The ability to pray from my spirit has transformed my life and ministry, and it can do the same for you. This practice also enhances my understanding and influences my other prayers. Those who devote time to praying in tongues can overcome any situation and gain access to God's divine wisdom.

I can give you an example of how using prayer language helped me succeed in my work. A company hired me to manage its global cybersecurity program, which involved a contract with the U.S. government. My job was to oversee the teams responsible for creating a secure computing environment that met the necessary security standards. Despite my lack of prior training or experience in this area, I took on the challenge, knowing the Holy Spirit would help me.

When I first joined the company, I found myself in meetings discussing topics beyond my expertise. Thankfully, I was given a private office where I could pray and seek guidance. After several weeks, I began to have ideas and insights that helped the team successfully complete the architectural design. Contractors and government officials were impressed with our work, not realizing that it resulted from my times praying in tongues and seeking interpretation from the Spirit. In essence, our entire program was an interpretation of tongues. You can do the same if you ask God for help; He does not play favorites. He sent His Spirit to guide all of His children.

I have met numerous ministers and Christians who believe it is not feasible to attain the same power that Jesus and the early church possessed. This belief has saddened me over the years. However, I hope you start recognizing how incorrect this viewpoint is. You have the Spirit of God within you, and He is eager to teach and guide you just as He has done for me. All you need to do is ask; you will find Him waiting and willing to work with you.

Chapter 28

Speaking God's Words to Release His Power

*Death and life are in the power of the tongue,
And those who love it will eat its fruit.*

PROVERBS 18:21

Our discussion in the previous chapters has referenced the spiritual prayer language accessible to all Christians. The initial mention of this language is found in Acts 2:4, where it states, "They were all filled with the Holy Spirit and began to speak with other tongues, as the Spirit gave them utterance." The Holy Spirit provided the words but did not physically speak through those in the upper room waiting for Him when He arrived on the day of Pentecost. Some individuals may have difficulty with this concept because they anticipate the Spirit initiating their speaking. It is also important to remember that you do not have to speak in tongues to be saved. We read in John 20:22 that Jesus appeared to the disciples after His resurrection and breathed the Spirit into their spirits. They were born again at that moment but were still instructed to "wait" for the Spirit before launching into ministry (Acts 1:4–5).

I want to continue our discussion about words from another angle. While we have been discussing how they relate to our lives, have you ever considered how God also uses words to unleash His power? The creation account in Genesis is a prime example. God used His words to create light. He continued to develop all other aspects of creation in the same manner. His power was released through the words He spoke. Genesis 1:2 says, "The Spirit of God was hovering over the face of the waters." I believe He was waiting for God's words before manifesting what was spoken. We will see in this chapter that He is still standing by, waiting for us to speak the Word of God today.

God's Creative Power Is in His Word

According to Hebrews 11:3, everything in existence was created by the power of God's spoken Word. This includes the earth, trees, and even the sun. The Holy Spirit acted in response to God's spoken Word, bringing all of creation into being. It's important to note that the things we "see" were not made from visible materials that can be perceived with our five physical senses but rather through the power of God's Word.

According to the Bible, God created everything we see around us by His Word. The first chapter of Genesis explains how God used His words to form the entire universe. The Word of God is constant and unchanging, and it was instrumental in releasing His creative power that formed the universe. Meditating on it and speaking it from a place of revelation knowledge can release the same power in your life. This is the message conveyed in Proverbs 18:21. God has given us the power to release either death or life with our tongues.

Satan's Focus Is the Word

In chapter 18, we learned that Satan targets the seed of God's Word that we plant in our hearts, and he tries to steal it before it can take root. This seed can release God's power, and Satan knows it. One of his most effective strategies is to distract us with formulas. I've come across people who have fallen into this trap and believe that just reading a verse out loud will release God's power. However, they don't understand the difference between acquired and revelation knowledge. Simply reciting God's Word won't release His power unless we speak it from a deep revelation imparted by the Spirit of God.

Hebrews 10:23 tells us we must "hold fast the confession of *our* hope without wavering." To unleash the power of God's Word, we must plant it in our souls and allow it time to produce a harvest of revelation knowledge by speaking the Word and meditating on it. The Spirit of God has personally guided me to read a verse aloud one hundred times in the past. This wasn't to claim the promise but to deeply ingrain the verse in my soul.

The Soil Brings Forth the Fruit

In Mark 4:28, Jesus shares a valuable lesson about the power of God's incorruptible seed. He explains that "the earth yields crops by itself." In this parable, the earth represents our souls. Once the seed of God's Word is planted within us, our soul immediately begins to cultivate it without any external force. The original text emphasizes that the soul is naturally inclined to do this without external influence. Unfortunately, we have the power to hinder this process by allowing Satan's distractions to divert our focus away from the Word.

Refuse to Let Go of Your Confession

To achieve victory, one must hold on to their profession of faith and be willing to stand firm. The results may not come immediately; sometimes, it may take days, months, or even years. However, if you remain steadfast until the end, God's Word will work within you and bring about the desired outcome.

Throughout the Scriptures, there is a recurring pattern of events. According to Hebrews 1:1, God communicated with the fathers through the prophets in the past. He always proclaimed His Word before taking any action. During the old covenant, only the prophet, priest, and king were anointed by the Spirit; therefore, the Word was conveyed through prophets. However, all believers presently have the Holy Spirit within them, who speaks directly to them without needing a prophet. The church has a prophetic office, which functions differently than its old covenant counterpart. We do not lean on it as God's people did before Jesus' earthly ministry.

Spoiled by the Traditions of Men

The power of God's Word, spoken from a renewed mind, can defeat Satan without any defense (Romans 12:2). Through His redemptive work, Jesus has already "disarmed" and made a public spectacle of him (Colossians 2:15). To exercise authority over Satan, we must meditate on the Word diligently until it renews our minds and grows in us.

In Colossians 2:8, Paul uses the term *cheat* to illustrate how Satan hunts down and captures his prey like a lion. This reminds me of Peter's warning that Satan prowls around "like a roaring lion," looking for someone to devour (1 Peter 5:8). Paul cautions his readers about the dangers of "philosophy and empty deceit, according to the tradition of men, according to the basic principles of the world," which are all tactics Satan uses to trap Christians.

We Are Upheld by the Word of God

According to the writer of Hebrews, God sustains all creation through His Word:

> God, who at various times and in various ways spoke in time past to the fathers by the prophets, has in these last days spoken to us by *His* Son, whom He has appointed heir of all things, through whom also He made the worlds; who being the brightness of *His* glory and the express image of His person, and upholding all things by the word of His power, when He had by Himself purged our sins, sat down at the right hand of the Majesty on high, having become so much better than the angels, as He has by inheritance obtained a more excellent name than they. (Hebrews 1:1–4)

Jesus, who is known as the living Word, created the universe and saved us from our sins. Everything in the universe results from God's Word, which is also why we can sense everything around us. It seems that many Christians are unaware of this fact. The words spoken by God during the creation of the universe keep everything running smoothly. There is no need for God to speak new words each day; the original Word spoken during creation continues to work and will never stop.

As believers, we have received the Word of God. This powerful message is like a seed that can take root in our souls. Over time, it can grow deep roots and transform our minds, as the Bible says in Romans 12:2. Once this happens, we can stand in the authority given to the church by Jesus and unleash God's creative power in our lives and the lives of those to whom we are called to minister.

Chapter 29

God's Word Is an Unchanging and Eternal Covenant

*"The grass withers, the flower fades,
But the word of our God stands forever."*

ISAIAH 40:8

Have you ever wondered why God allows so many bad things to happen in the world? I used to be bothered by reading the news and seeing all the horrible things happening around me. Murder rates are climbing, crime is seemingly out of control, babies are born out of wedlock, and the biblical standard for marriage has become the exception rather than the rule. From a purely natural perspective, lawlessness has become the norm globally.

The Holy Spirit has opened my eyes over the years. God is not causing these things to happen. We live in a world tainted by the sin of Adam and Eve. I have heard ministers and Christians talk about God being in control. He did not make the first couple partake of the forbidden fruit, leading to the fall of humanity. They were given free will, just as we are today. We cannot blame Him for the fruit that grows from the corruptible seeds we've allowed in our lives.

Do Not Let Your Heart Be Troubled

One day, as I was thinking about the increasing darkness in the world, the Holy Spirit reminded me of Jesus' instructions to His disciples in John 14:1: "Let not your heart be troubled." I have often heard this statement quoted by ministers and Christians over the years. Few consider the context in which Jesus said it. He was beginning His last significant discourse to the disciples before the crucifixion. John's fourteenth, fifteenth, and sixteenth chapters contain Jesus' last words to them before His death. He began with a warning not to let their hearts be disturbed by what they experienced when He was arrested, tried, beaten, whipped, crucified, and buried. That seems like a tall order, doesn't it?

So, in light of Jesus' statement, is it possible to live in such a lawless society without being troubled by it? I would say yes, and He shows us how to do so in John 14:2–3:

> "In My Father's house are many mansions; if *it were* not *so*, I would have told you. I go to prepare a place for you. And if I go and prepare a place for you, I will come again and receive you to Myself; that where I am, *there* you may be also. And where I go you know, and the way you know."

Notice that Jesus immediately began speaking about heaven. He instructed His disciples to keep their minds fixed on God through everything they were about to experience. We walk through the darkness around us without allowing our hearts to be troubled in the same way today. The Word of God is eternal, and you will find yourself experiencing less and less anxiety the more deeply it becomes implanted in your soul.

God's Power Is Released through Our Words

Every word of God is eternal. The words He released to create the universe are recorded in Genesis. They continue to work today just as every word He has uttered since continues to work. This means we can have complete confidence in every word recorded in the Bible. You can take any promise from Scripture and have full assurance that it will release His power into your life when you release it with your tongue.

If you release the Word of God with your tongue, it will work for you twenty-four hours a day. It will continue working unless you release words contrary to the promise. An example is people who receive prayer from a minister in church for healing. Prayer consists of words released over the sickness or disease that will release God's healing power if offered in faith. The power begins to work immediately regardless of whether an immediate change occurs. Many people cause it to go dormant by releasing counterwords such as, "I don't feel any different, so the prayer must not have worked."

Faith and Patience

A word of caution is in order at this point. Becoming deeply rooted in God's Word and moving into revelation knowledge takes time. We are often willing to release our faith for just an instant. We will become discouraged and begin to waver if time passes without any physical manifestation to prove the answer has been provided. You must be willing to stand on the promises of God for whatever time is necessary to see the desired answer manifest.

God can override the process by working a miracle, but that is not how He normally provides. Miracles are crisis-oriented. He desires for us to live on a higher level, walking in victory to the point where miracles are not needed except in rare circumstances. The challenge, though, is that we struggle with patience, so most do not want to stand in faith until victory manifests.

I cannot tell you what things don't always manifest instantly, but I wish I could. There are some things we will not understand in this life. The one thing I can say, though, is the answer will come if you do not stop it. You are the only one who can stop the manifestation, and you do so with your words. Satan cannot prevent the manifestation from occurring if he cannot get you to speak words that cause your faith to wither and die or go dormant.

Speaking Things into Existence

The Word of God is firmly established in heaven and remains unchanging. It can bring about change and release His power in your life. However, speaking words that contradict its promises can render it powerless. Many people are unaware of this and fail to control their words. By examining the creation account, we can better understand how this process works.

> Then God said, "Let there be light"; and there was light. And God saw the light, that it was good; and God divided the light from the darkness. God called the light Day, and the darkness He called Night. So the evening and the morning were the first day. (Genesis 1:3–5)

God created light and darkness with His words. As we saw earlier, He spoke them into existence!

> Then God said, "Let there be lights in the firmament of the heavens to divide the day from the night; and let them be for signs and seasons, and for days and years; and let them be for lights in the firmament of the heavens to give light on the earth"; and it was so. Then God made two great lights: the greater light to rule the day, and the lesser light to rule the night. He made the stars also. God set them in the firmament of the heavens to

give light on the earth, and to rule over the day and over the night, and to divide the light from the darkness. And God saw that it was good. So the evening and the morning were the fourth day. (Genesis 1:14–19)

Every word spoken by God contains power and can be considered a seed filled with His authority (1 Peter 1:23). Unlike humans, who may say one thing and do another, God always keeps His word. We can trust that if God has promised something, He will make it happen because He is not a man who lies. Every word He speaks is significant and carries weight. People today do not hold words in the same respect as the early church, but we can be assured that God's words are never empty or vain. We see this in Numbers 23:19:

> "God *is* not a man, that He should lie,
> Nor a son of man, that He should repent.
> Has He said, and will He not do?
> Or has He spoken, and will He not make it good?"

God cannot break His Word. It is His covenant between Himself and mankind. If you are not familiar with this term, it simply means a contract. He has established a contract between us and ratified it with the blood of Jesus. You can rest assured that He will abide by it. Can He be assured of the same for the words we speak?

God's Word Is His Covenant

God's Word is a covenant between Him and creation. The passages from Genesis provide an example of this. We also see this in Jeremiah 33:25–26:

> Thus says the Lord: "If My covenant is not with day and night, and if I have not appointed the ordinances of

heaven and earth, then I will cast away the descendants of Jacob and David My servant, so that I will not take any of his descendants to be rulers over the descendants of Abraham, Isaac, and Jacob. For I will cause their captives to return, and will have mercy on them."

God gave these words to Jeremiah to assure Israel of their covenant with Him. He wanted them to know it was as firm as His commitment to govern the "day and night." Malachi 3:6 tells us He is the Lord and He will not change. You can be just as assured of His commitment to His Word today as Israel could. We can be just as confident as Jeremiah that God is "ready to perform" His Word in our lives (Jeremiah 1:12).

Chapter 30

God's Word and the Anointing

Since you have purified your souls in obeying the truth through the Spirit in sincere love of the brethren, love one another fervently with a pure heart, having been born again, not of corruptible seed but incorruptible, through the word of God which lives and abides forever, because

> *"All flesh is as grass,*
> *And all the glory of man as the flower of the grass.*
> *The grass withers,*
> *And its flower falls away,*
> *But the word of the* L ORD *endures forever."*

Now this is the word which by the gospel was preached to you.

1 PETER 1:22–25

Christians spend countless hours crying out to God, pleading with Him to pour out His power in our services. However, there is no evidence the early church prayed this way. The one example I do see of them praying for the Lord to work with them is found in Acts 4:29–30:

> "Lord, look on their threats, and grant to Your servants that with all boldness they may speak Your word, by stretching out Your hand to heal, and that signs and wonders may be done through the name of Your holy Servant Jesus."

Peter and John were imprisoned and then released after being commanded "not to speak at all nor teach in the name of Jesus" (Acts 4:18). They immediately went to where their friends were gathered and joined them in prayer. We should note that they did not pray for God to intervene or pour out His power. Instead, they prayed for "boldness" to speak the Word of God. I think our reaction to imprisonment would be much different today.

The Anointing Resides in Your Heart

I have attended many prayer meetings over the years. The focus was usually on petitioning God for His anointing or outpouring His Spirit. We prayed with sincere hearts but did so in ignorance. The anointing we sought is deposited in the heart of every Christian when they accept Jesus and are made new creations in Him (2 Corinthians 5:17). John refers to this in 1 John 2:27:

> But the anointing which you have received from Him abides in you, and you do not need that anyone teach you; but as the same anointing teaches you concerning all things, and is true, and is not a lie, and just as it has taught you, you will abide in Him.

According to John, the anointing "abides" in us, meaning it has established itself permanently within our souls and exerts its power over us. This anointing was received when Jesus "breathed" the Holy Spirit into our spirits (John 20:22) and will continue to remain there. We do not need to pray or cry out to God for it to be sent.

Anointing Is an Outgrowth of Our Fellowship with the Spirit

According to John, the anointing of God is not an intangible force but something that "abides" within us, similar to the Holy Spirit. The degree of anointing we experience depends on how much time we spend fellowshipping with the Spirit.

Moses spent more than forty days with God on Mount Sinai. When he returned to the Israeli camp, his face glowed with the glory of God, and he had to cover it (Exodus 34:29–35). There is no indication that Moses fasted or prayed for this to happen. The glory emanated from within him because he spent time in the presence of God.

Christians don't need to pray for God's anointing because that request implies doubt in John's statement that it already exists within us. According to Paul's words in 2 Corinthians 13:14, anyone who believes in Jesus has access to the "communion of the Holy Spirit." As you spend more time nurturing your relationship with the Holy Spirit, you will experience a more tangible anointing.

The Holy Spirit Is Our Teacher

According to Peter, we are reborn through God's Word, which he calls the "incorruptible" seed (1 Peter 1:23). We receive this Word through our ears when we hear it being taught or preached (Romans 10:17). Jesus compares the spreading of God's Word to a sower planting seeds in the parable of the sower (Mark 4:14), which we've mentioned before. Essentially, the Word enters our soul through our ears as we listen to it being spoken.

You possess more of God's anointing within you than you may realize. To tap into this anointing, it's crucial to spend time with the Holy Spirit. According to Jesus, the Spirit will dwell within us and teach us all things, reminding us of the Lord's words (John 14:17, 26). By spending time alone with the Holy Spirit, we allow Him to impart revelation knowledge of the incorruptible seed planted in our hearts. As we have seen in previous chapters, it's helpful to dedicate time each day to praying in the Spirit to speed up this process.

The Word Is Satan's Target

The relationship between God's Word, the Holy Spirit, and anointing is closely connected. The Holy Spirit's purpose is to provide revelation knowledge, and He uses the Word to do so. When we spend time in fellowship with Him, we receive this knowledge, and anointing is an outgrowth of this time spent together. In Mark 4:15–20, Jesus shares a parable about the sower, illustrating Satan's efforts to stop the Word from taking root in our souls:

> "And these are the ones by the wayside where the word is sown. When they hear, Satan comes immediately and takes away the word that was sown in their hearts. These likewise are the ones sown on stony ground who, when they hear the word, immediately receive it with gladness; and they have no root in themselves, and so endure only for a time. Afterward, when tribulation or persecution arises for the word's sake, immediately they stumble. Now these are the ones sown among thorns; *they are* the ones who hear the word, and the cares of this world, the deceitfulness of riches, and the desires for other things entering in choke the word, and it becomes unfruitful. But these are the ones sown on good ground, those who hear the word, accept *it,* and bear fruit: some thirtyfold, some sixty, and some a hundred."

The Word of God is planted in the soil of our souls. However, the enemy will try to target the Word before it can take root. Satan will use any means possible to steal the seed of God's Word before it has a chance to become firmly established within us.

Trials, Afflictions, and the Word of God

It's important to remember that Satan doesn't care about you. Instead, he fears the power of the Word and its ability to transform your soul (Romans 12:2; James 1:21), which can allow God's power to flow through you to those you minister to. According to Paul, the battle against Satan is primarily fought within your soul (2 Corinthians 10:3–6). Jesus also warned us of the "tribulation" and "persecution" that may arise due to the Word planted in our souls (Matthew 13:21). *Tribulation* refers to the internal pressures in our souls that may try to steer us away from the Word. *Persecution* paints a vivid image of a hunt aimed at taking down a person like an animal. This brings to mind Peter's comparison of Satan to "a roaring lion," constantly on the prowl, seeking anyone to devour (1 Peter 5:8). Satan will incite others to attack you, but it's important not to take it personally. His ultimate goal is to prevent the Word from taking root in your heart.

The Earth Produces the Crop

Jesus placed the responsibility for seed growth on the ground:

> And He said, "The kingdom of God is as if a man should scatter seed on the ground, and should sleep by night and rise by day, and the seed should sprout and grow, he himself does not know how. For the earth yields crops by itself: first the blade, then the head, after that the full grain in the head. But when the grain ripens, immediately he puts in the sickle, because the harvest has come." (Mark 4:26–29)

In verse 28, we see that the earth has the power to make any seed planted in it grow. This includes God's Word, which is similar to natural seeds that require watering. To water God's Word, we spend time with the Holy Spirit, yielding to His utterances in prayer. It is important to allow the Word to take root and be nurtured by the Holy Spirit, which happens during our private moments with Him. As we spend time alone with Him, the anointing will naturally develop and become evident to everyone, just like it did for Moses after leaving God's presence.

We don't have to produce results; that's not our responsibility. Although, sometimes, our egos and physical bodies might think otherwise. Our task is to plant God's seed and follow His Spirit. It will take time and effort, but if we devote time every day to these things, we'll see God's Word grow deep roots within us and witness manifestations of power. There'll be resistance, but we'll come out of every struggle as winners.

Seek First the Word of God

In Paul's teachings, he explains that those who are focused on their physical senses rather than the Word of God are on a path that leads to death (Romans 8:6). This is a common path that many people choose to take, where they prioritize things like education, skin color, or economic status, even though these things hold no significance to God. It's important to understand that God has the ability to bless anyone, regardless of their education level or skin color, whether they live in an affluent area or in the ghetto.

To fully follow God's plan, we must prioritize His Word in our lives. Jesus taught His disciples that those who abide in His Word will experience true spiritual freedom (John 8:31–32). This requires us to focus solely on it. While we cannot walk at God's level of faith, the Word empowers us to unleash His anointing and creative power, just as He did when He spoke the universe into existence (Genesis 1). I think this is what Paul meant when he said, "The life which I now live in the flesh I live by the faith in the Son of God" (Galatians 2:20). The Greek text reveals that he was referring to the faith provided by God, which is granted to all believers when they first hear the Word of God and make Jesus their Lord and Savior (Romans 10:17; 12:3).

Chapter 31

Plant the Word and Defend It

> *Then Jesus, being filled with the Holy Spirit, returned from the Jordan and was led by the Spirit into the wilderness, being tempted for forty days by the devil. And in those days He ate nothing, and afterward, when they had ended, He was hungry. And the devil said to Him, "If You are the Son of God, command this stone to become bread." But Jesus answered him, saying, "It is written, 'Man shall not live by bread alone, but by every word of God.'" Then the devil, taking Him up on a high mountain, showed Him all the kingdoms of the world in a moment of time. And the devil said to Him, "All this authority I will give You, and their glory; for this has been delivered to me, and I give it to whomever I wish. Therefore, if You will worship before me, all will be Yours." And Jesus answered and said to him, "Get behind Me, Satan! For it is written, 'You shall worship the LORD your God, and Him only you shall serve.'" Then he brought Him to Jerusalem, set Him on the pinnacle of the temple, and said to Him, "If You are the Son of God, throw Yourself down from here. For it is written: 'He shall give His angels charge over you, To keep you,' and 'In their hands they shall bear you up, Lest you dash your foot against a stone.'" And Jesus answered and said to him, "It has been said, 'You shall not tempt the LORD your God.'" Now when the devil had ended every temptation, he departed from Him until an opportune time. Then Jesus returned in the power of the Spirit to Galilee, and news of Him went out through all the surrounding region. And He taught in their synagogues, being glorified by all.*

LUKE 4:1–15

The account of Jesus' temptation shows that Satan's focus was on the Word of God. His intention was to make Jesus doubt what God had said, but Jesus used the Word to respond. He said, "It is written," and successfully overcame each temptation. You can do the same, but it's important to take the time to allow the Word to become deeply rooted in your heart.

According to John and Luke, Jesus was the incarnation of the Word of God, brought about by the Holy Spirit's power. Every word Jesus spoke carried the authority of God. Yet even when tempted by Satan, Jesus chose to quote the written Word rather than add His own thoughts. If the living Word of God could not improve upon what was already written, neither can we. You can depend on and trust the Word to pave the way to victory in every situation. You must commit to meditate on it until it develops deep roots and the Holy Spirit can impart revelation knowledge.

Defending the Word from Your Place of Revelation

When faced with the devil's temptations, Jesus used God's Word as His weapon of choice. You can do the same when your response to Satan comes from revelation knowledge and not acquired knowledge. We looked at the account of the seven sons of Sceva (Acts 19:13–16). They tried to cast a demon out based on what they had seen and heard Paul doing. The demon beat them and sent them running down the street naked! Jesus emerged victorious over the enemy's temptations because He responded from revelation. If you follow His example, you will experience the same levels of victory.

The book of Revelation teaches us that we can defeat Satan by relying on the blood of the Lamb and the word of our testimony (Revelations 12:11). Additionally, in Revelation 19, we learn that when Jesus returns, He will use the power of His words to overthrow the nations of the world. This power of speech is the strongest force in existence; God used it to create the universe, and Jesus used it to resist Satan's temptations. You, too, can use this power to overcome any afflictions and hardships you may face.

Are You Willing to Pay the Price?

Jesus relied on God's Word to resist the devil's temptations. We, too, can use this powerful weapon if we fill our hearts with it and spend time with the Holy Spirit to gain revelation knowledge. When we speak the Word from a place of revelation, Satan is powerless against its might.

The power of God is contained in the Word of God. However, this power cannot be unleashed unless we mix the Word with faith (Hebrews 4:2). To mix the Word with faith, we must first plant it in our souls and allow it to grow into revelation knowledge. Ultimately, it is up to you to decide whether or not you are willing to invest the time and effort necessary to immerse yourself in the Word until this occurs.

To walk in the power of God, you must be committed and steadfast. The Holy Spirit cannot do this for you. You must choose whether or not to invest your time, effort, and energy in pursuing the Word. It will require sacrificing certain activities like watching TV, attending sporting events, and keeping up with daily news. We believe that, by reading this far, you have shown willingness. Our team is praying for your journey and expecting nothing but success!

God Desires More for Your Life

The printed Word of God is a perfect representation of God's Word. You can carry it under your arm and appear religious in church, but God's Word will not produce His power until it is first planted in your heart, as we've seen. I keep repeating this because I've visited many Christians whose homes are filled with Bibles, and still, they are living powerless lives filled with sickness and lack. You do not need to be one of these. The Word is the vehicle that will carry you out of everyday struggles into the victory Christ gave you on the cross.

As we have seen, the power flow begins when we plant the Word of God in our hearts. We give it time to grow once planted and nurture it through times of fellowship with the Spirit and praying in tongues over the seed. Far too many have yet to expend the necessary effort for the Word to produce anything but acquired knowledge. As one preacher once said, we have become a church of empty hearts and full heads. The Word is preached, but it goes in one ear and then out the other. God desires so much more for our lives.

The Choice Is Yours to Make

To honor the Word and protect our hearts, we should follow the guidance provided in Proverbs 4:20–22.

> My son, give attention to my words;
> Incline your ear to my sayings.
> Do not let them depart from your eyes;
> Keep them in the midst of your heart;
> For they *are* life to those who find them,
> And health to all their flesh.
>   (Proverbs 4:20–22)

To truly internalize the teachings of the Bible, each individual must plant the Word in their own heart. Though God has made His Word accessible, it is our choice whether or not to put in the effort to sow it in our hearts. Once we do, we must also protect it from Satan's attempts to steal it.

Some Christians attribute everything to God "being in control," but this mindset does not align with the responsibility of safeguarding the Word of God. It is easier to blame external factors for our problems instead of taking accountability for our lack of focus on God's teachings.

Final Words

To truly defend the Word of God, it's better to not listen to it at all than to listen and do nothing. I'm not suggesting you refute everyone who disagrees with you, but rather, protect the Word already planted in your heart. If you spend your time listening to criticism or watching TV, you're not doing your heart any favors. Instead, you must guard what you allow into your eyes and ears so that the Word will thrive.

In 1 Timothy 6:12, Paul advised Timothy to "fight the good fight of faith" and "lay hold on eternal life." He knew that achieving success in the Christian walk requires a readiness to fight. The adversary will employ all the tools at his disposal to prevent the Word from taking hold in your heart. He will try to snatch it away before it can take root, thus preventing you from gaining revelation knowledge.

According to Jude, living a victorious Christian life requires actively defending your faith:

> Beloved, while I was very diligent to write to you concerning our common salvation, I found it necessary to write to you exhorting you to contend earnestly for the faith which was once for all delivered to the saints. For certain men have crept in unnoticed, who long ago were marked out for this condemnation, ungodly men, who turn the grace of our God into lewdness and deny the only Lord God and our Lord Jesus Christ. (Jude 1:3–4)

Jude's letter aimed to encourage readers to defend their faith with earnestness. Our faith is a precious gift received at salvation, and it's our responsibility to safeguard it. Unfortunately, many Christians overlook this truth. We need to store the Word in our hearts and protect it. While it's our duty to keep it safe, God will equip us with all the necessary resources.

As we conclude this book, I want to reiterate that there are no shortcuts when it comes to spiritual matters. The Word of God won't become a part of us overnight. We have to read it, confess it, and spend time meditating on it. God has sent His Holy Spirit to guide us, but we need to be receptive to His teachings. He's always there to support us on our journey.

www.ingramcontent.com/pod-product-compliance
Lightning Source LLC
LaVergne TN
LVHW041934070526
838199LV00051BA/2789